DIY
Credit Builder

Beginners' Guide to Building Credit

How to build credit at 18 (or any age) and understand credit, budgeting, credit disputes, credit reports, credit utilization ratio, and the power of a high credit score

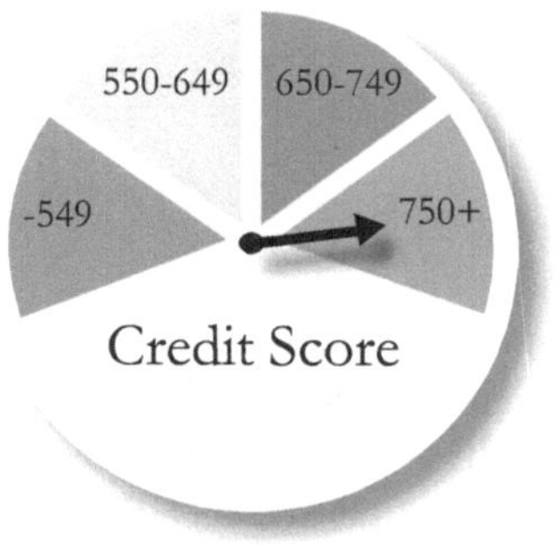

Kendyl Jameson

The End Result

ISBN: 978-0-9992498-4-0

Library of Congress Control Number: 2021915629

Cover art by Kendyl Jameson.

Visit KendylJameson.com and download the free credit builder workbook.

Publisher's Cataloging-in-Publication Data
Names: Jameson, Kendyl, author.
Title: DIY credit builder : beginners' guide to building credit / Kendyl Jameson.
Description: Delray Beach, FL: The End Result, 2021.
Identifiers: LCCN: 2021915629 | ISBN: 978-0-9992498-4-0 (paperback)
Subjects: LCSH Consumer credit--United States--Handbooks, manuals, etc. | Finance, Personal--United States--Handbooks, manuals, etc. | Credit ratings--United States. | Credit bureaus--United States. | Consumer protection--Law and legislation--United States. | BISAC BUSINESS & ECONOMICS / Personal Finance / Money Management
Classification: LCC HG3756.U54 .J363 2021 | DDC 332.7/43--dc23

Other books by Kendyl Jameson

Scan the QR code next to each title to access the book's full description and details online. When the QR code is scanned, your device will open the relevant title on Amazon.

The Pirates of My Soul:
A Transformational Voyage to Self-Empowerment

DIY Credit Repair:
Beginners' Guide to Credit Repair

DIY Reparación de Crédito:
Guía del principiante para la reparación del crédito

CONTENTS

INTRODUCTION 1

DO I NEED CREDIT? 3
- Why Credit Is Necessary
- Cash, Credit, Or Debit

BENEFITS OF CREDIT 6
- Better Opportunities With Credit
- Better Interest & Approval Rates

TYPES OF CREDIT 9
- What Is Consumer Credit?
- Loan Or Line Of Credit
- Credit Cards
- Secured & Unsecured

APPLYING FOR CREDIT 14
- Credit Language
- Looking For A Creditor
- The Application Process
- Credit Check

CREDIT INQUIRIES 20
- Hard Inquiry
- Soft Inquiry
- Prescreened Offers

CREDIT REPORTS 24
- Credit Report Already Exists
- Ordering & Reviewing A Credit Report
- Reported Accounts
- Credit Report Discrepancies

PRE-APPLICATION PREP 34
- Do Account Status & Details Matter?
- Prepare Before Applying
- Squeeze Here For More Credit

INTEREST & APR 43
Interest Rate & Annual Percentage Rate (APR)
Fixed & Variable Interest Rates
Lowering High Rates
Zero Percent Offers

BUDGETING & PAYMENTS 49
Why Should I Budget?
Account Analysis
Top Priority Accounts

GET STARTED 59
Student Loans
Personal Loans
Auto Loans
Department Store Credit Cards
Starter Credit Cards
Major Credit Cards

CREDIT SCORES & CUR 69
Credit Scores
Credit Score Breakdown
Variables & Credit Utilization Ratio (CUR)
Closing An Account

CREDIT DISPUTES 76
What To Look For
Fixing Credit Report Errors
Credit Dispute Letters

CREDIT THREATS 84
Mail Or Online Fraud
SIM Swap Fraud
Skimming & Shimming
Social Engineering
Unauthorized Charges
Protect Your Identity

CONCLUSION 96

ABOUT THE AUTHOR 99

INTRODUCTION

This guide to building credit is ideal for people beginning or improving their independent financial situation. Readers who will gain the most from this include teenagers, college students, individuals new to the credit system in the United States, and anyone else who needs to establish or improve their credit.

Easy to read and understand, *DIY Credit Builder: Beginners' Guide to Building Credit* covers all the credit basics and more. This guide explores the concept of credit and how it works, why it's necessary, how to get it, how to use it, and how to keep it.

Credit is complicated and while reading this, you will notice topics are intertwined within each other. Therefore, I suggest reading the book in its entirety before moving forward.

This information will be useful throughout your life. As times change, some of the aspects and forms of credit will vary but credit itself isn't going anywhere. And as our country moves toward becoming a cashless society, it will become more important than ever.

Therefore, having great credit and a high credit score will always be worthy goals. But credit can be fickle, so it's best to nourish and protect it while watching it grow.

When you have established some credit, you will need to monitor it, ensuring that all activity is yours and properly handled. But don't worry, along with a bunch of other important topics, this is also covered to put you on the right track.

This book is based on my experience of building, then repairing, and now maintaining an exciting credit rating. And although I have experienced financial hardships, it was my credit that saved me every time.

After building excellent credit in college, an economic downturn within a year of graduation changed my course. With it, I lost my job and my new home. I was forced to live off of my credit, using credit cards to pay for everything. This was my first financial crisis and, thanks to my credit, I was able to survive.

However, due to an ongoing recession coupled with the loss of income, I couldn't keep up with the payments. My credit was going downhill and I was in a financial bind.

It was during this time when others recommended filing for bankruptcy. But rather than taking that route, I chose to repair and rebuild my credit. Although it was challenging, it was also educational and rewarding. And what I learned and applied then is how I have maintained an impressive credit score to this day without faltering.

The truth is, what happened to me can happen to anyone. And that is why it is important to set yourself up to be in a better position tomorrow than today. I know that if you invest the time now, it will serve you well in your future.

The sooner you start building a solid payment pattern for excellent credit, the sooner you can take advantage of perks associated with being financially responsible. And although it takes time to do it correctly, don't let that put you off.

I promise the process will be educational, possibly fun, and definitely rewarding. And before you know it, you'll be flexing your credit muscle!

Great credit is vital for better financial opportunities.

Chapter 1

DO I NEED CREDIT?

If you have never had credit before, you might be wondering if you need it, and if so, why.

Credit plays an important role in our daily lives here in the United States. The sooner you begin establishing credit, the sooner you can enjoy the conveniences it provides. Many people assume credit is merely a tool used to buy things, but it reaches beyond the power to purchase.

Why Credit Is Necessary

It's true that building excellent credit will take time. However, unless you can pay cash for everything, including all major purchases, credit is necessary. A few examples of when you'll need it are: taking out a personal loan, renting a place to live, buying appliances, a car, house or furniture, and starting a business.

As you can see, whether for a place to live or to purchase your favorite big-ticket items with fewer restrictions, credit plays a major part. Therefore, a high credit score and solid payment history will always prove beneficial.

When applying for credit, potential creditors will follow a process before approving any terms. And it doesn't matter if it's for a line of credit such as for a credit card or to rent space, such as an apartment.

Generally, they begin by requesting a copy of your credit report, also referred to as a credit file, from the credit bureaus. This is because your credit history is tracked by credit bureaus and revealed within the report.

After careful review of your report and the completed application, creditors will determine if you are an acceptable risk.

Very seldom will you have the opportunity to obtain a loan or line of credit without going through this process. Hence my belief that everyone should make their credit a financial priority.

Cash, Credit, Or Debit

I love paying with cash whenever possible. It is an excellent way to avoid creating debt and having to pay for things after the thrill is gone.

Cash and debit cards are especially useful for smaller purchases, like that morning cup of coffee from your favorite barista or bag of chips from the convenience store. But these small purchases add up quickly. If they are all charged to a credit card, the result is often owing more than expected when the bill arrives.

However, there are times when it could be more beneficial to use a credit card than cash or a debit card. To begin with, it is an excellent way to build credit. Here are a few examples where using a credit card instead of a cash alternative could save you money:

» Cash back on purchases;

» Discounts on categories assigned by creditor;

» Discounts on purchases made with store's credit card; and

» Receiving points or discounts on travel.

If you already have a credit card or two (or when you do), be aware of which card offers which perks and promotions, and when. Keeping track of your cards' offers will help you determine when purchasing on credit is better than paying with cash and vice versa.

To build credit, you do have to use it. But it's important to practice self-restraint to not max out your credit lines. The key, as with anything, is to use it in moderation and pay attention to what you're doing.

Once buried in debt, it can take years to repay and cost far more than anticipated.

I would be remiss if I did not mention here the importance of monitoring debit card transactions.

If you prefer using a debit card for most of your purchases, monitor your account and keep track of all transactions. One forgotten or overlooked purchase could create an avalanche of problems. This is especially true if you rely on automatic payments and accidentally overdraw from your account. The resulting fees can be costly.

In summary, whether you are planning to borrow money for a major purchase now or at some point in the future, you will need credit. And because it plays a major role in how we structure our lives, you may as well start building credit now so when you need it, it will be there.

Chapter 2

BENEFITS OF CREDIT

One of the best benefits of having credit is being able to obtain things. These things may be physical items or opportunities. Either way, the better your credit, the better your odds of being approved and often, at a better price or rate.

Better Opportunities With Credit

In general, when people think about having good credit, it's for buying things such as new clothes, a car, or a house. And of course, that's part of it. But, it's also important to acknowledge how credit makes opportunities possible.

Take for example, renting an apartment. For most of us, there are areas where we would prefer to live. Maybe closer to the center of town for easier access to nightlife and shopping. Or, possibly closer to work for a shorter commute.

Whichever it is, the more desirable the location, usually the higher the rent. The higher the rent, the harder it is to qualify for the lease and the more particular the landlord will be.

In a situation like this, having excellent credit can help you qualify for something better suited to your desired lifestyle and possibly beat the competition. Even though someone else might have the money to move in, they'll also need a solid payment history. If they do not have the latter and you do, you could be the more desirable tenant.

Another example of how having great credit can create opportunities is with credit itself.

The better your payment history with a creditor, the more credit they will be willing to extend your way. Should you need more credit on an existing line of credit or need to take out a loan, the better your chances of getting what you want.

Keeping this in mind, it is easy to see how credit makes opportunities possible that may otherwise be off limits.

Better Interest & Approval Rates

There are two things no one wants to deal with when they need to take out a loan or line of credit: high interest rates and rejection.

Having great credit can relieve both of these in most situations. I say most because, as with everything, there are always exceptions.

Therefore, the better your credit score and proven credit history, the better your chances of being approved. This also increases your odds for a lower interest rate on that loan or line of credit. Following is an example of this playing out in an everyday situation.

True Story:

Recently, a reader shared this story and I think it fits well. In the past, they had read my book, *DIY Credit Repair: Beginners' Guide to Credit Repair* and followed the suggestions. After diligently applying themselves, they had successfully repaired their credit, raising their credit score from the low 600's to 820. Very impressive, indeed!

Now, with an excellent credit score in hand, they headed off with confidence to buy a new car for $25,000. When the dealership first offered the loan, it was at 4.5% for 60 months.

With these terms and using the full 60 months to pay off the loan, the monthly payment would be $466 and the total cost of the loan $27,965. Not the best, but not the worst either.

However, the dealership had yet to examine their credit history. After reviewing their credit report, the offer improved substantially. And before it was finalized, the new loan details were adjusted to 1.5% for 72 months.

Now, the new monthly payment is $363 and, if they use the full 72 months allowed to pay off the loan, it will cost them a total of $26,157.

In this example, the borrower immediately saved $103 per month that can be used for other expenses, with an overall savings of $1,808. And if they make additional interest-only payments, they will not only pay the loan off sooner, but also save more money.

Then came one more surprise. Their amazing credit earned them a lower rate on the insurance, and that made the purchase even sweeter.

This purchase experience is an excellent example of the benefits of having great credit.

Of course, having amazing credit does not guarantee you will always get what you want the way you want it. There will always be other factors, including your income and possibly length of time at your job.

But it can definitely save you money and open other financial doors. And although your fabulous credit won't eliminate interest rates entirely, if a zero percent option is available, you would at least be in the running to receive it.

Hopefully by this point, you can see the importance of taking the time to build excellent credit. Through these practical examples, I trust you understand there is much to be gained by investing the energy in nurturing your credit for your financial future.

And now that we've established that, let's cover a few more topics before moving on to how to build credit at 18—or any age!

Chapter 3

TYPES OF CREDIT

When exploring the bits and pieces of credit, certain words and terms will often reappear. Some topics will pop up in other areas as well, but that is not meant to be redundant.

It's how the industry has evolved over time, with words and phrases being applied to incorporate the new with the old. You will notice the overlap in this chapter and, as stated in the Introduction, throughout this guide.

What Is Consumer Credit?

Consumer credit, also referred to as consumer debt, is credit granted to consumers to make purchases. There are two kinds of consumer credit: revolving and installment.

Revolving credit is an open line of credit with a predetermined maximum amount available that the borrower can use, pay off, and use again. These accounts generally have a higher annual percentage rate (APR), and the minimum amount due is a percentage of the balance owed. A credit card is a perfect example of revolving credit.

Installment credit is a loan of a set amount provided, often to purchase an item. A loan generally has a lower annual percentage rate with a fixed payment amount for a predetermined number of payments. An auto loan is an example of installment credit.

Loan Or Line Of Credit

A loan is a set amount borrowed in full with a predetermined due date and interest rate. If you want to borrow $10,000, you would borrow all of it at once, even if you never use it all.

With a loan, the interest begins accruing immediately on the entire amount. However, with many loans (not all), when additional payments are made to the principal only, then the loan may be paid off earlier than originally planned. Either way, when the loan is paid off, it's done. A mortgage is an example of a loan.

A line of credit is a set amount that can be borrowed in increments or in full. The creditor establishes the maximum amount that can be borrowed. If the amount awarded by the creditor is $10,000, then that is the credit line.

Now when you have a zero balance on this new line of credit and use $500 in one billing cycle, your statement will reflect that you owe $500 and the available credit is $9,500. When you pay the $500 in full before the due date, the credit line is restored and the available credit will be $10,000 again. This is a revolving line of credit.

Two examples of a revolving line of credit are the home equity line and credit card. Credit cards are the most accessible, as you need to have a home before you can apply for a home equity line.

Credit Cards

Credit cards are issued by banks, gas stations, department stores, and other retailers. Credit cards provide a revolving line of credit at an amount and annual percentage rate determined by the creditor.

Most cards offer perks, rewards, and other benefits. Knowing which package suits your needs and lifestyle the most will help you decide which card(s) provide the best benefits.

For those who do not have any credit yet, these perks may not matter. The truth is, you have to start somewhere, regardless of how much you can get back from using the card.

Take the typical department store credit card. Most are restricted to that particular store. If you shop there only during the holidays, will it benefit you to apply for one of their cards? Probably not.

However, during checkout, you might be asked if you want to apply for one and save a percentage of your total purchase that day. But there's no guarantee you will be approved. Nor does it mean it's a good choice, if you don't shop there often.

An exception to this is if you are starting to build credit from scratch. If you don't have any existing credit or credit cards and need to get something going, then a department store credit card might be the way to go.

If this is the route you choose, try to find a store you will purchase from several times a year. The idea behind establishing credit is that you show consistency in paying your bills. If you make one purchase a year on the card and pay it off when due, it will take years to show a payment pattern.

Determine if you need credit before applying. If so, does this particular option suit you?

Bank or credit union credit cards (for our purposes, major credit cards), are more widely accepted than most retail credit cards. And the best place to start is where you already have an account. Your financial institution knows your history and is usually the most willing to offer their customers credit through a credit card or loan.

But wait a minute. My bank said I need a secured credit card or loan. What is that all about?

If this is you, don't panic. When a borrower has yet to establish a positive payment history, the lender often requires a secured account.

But that's okay. At least there is an option and they haven't slammed the door shut. Therefore, using a secured account is an excellent tool for anyone who needs to build and establish credit.

Secured & Unsecured

The term secured refers to the borrower guaranteeing repayment with something tangible. For a secured loan, the guarantee is made by posting collateral such as equipment, jewelry, a house, car, or other valuables.

Simple examples are buying a house or car. In either case, the lender holds the title until the mortgage or auto loan is paid off. And because they hold the title, the borrower cannot sell the house or vehicle without first paying off the balance of the loan.

You've probably heard of homes going into foreclosure and cars being repossessed. These situations occur when the borrower has defaulted on their loan and the creditor reclaims the asset in an attempt to clear the debt. As you can see, borrowing is a serious obligation.

Mortgages and auto loans are secured loans.

For a secured credit card, the borrower deposits money into the account, which then determines the amount of credit available to borrow. That said, a deposit of $300 will grant the borrower a revolving line of credit up to a maximum of $300.

With a secured credit card, you are lending yourself the money. But because you already have the money, that's not why you do it.

Remember, the first goal is to build credit. And the only way to do it is to prove to a creditor that you are capable of repaying a debt as promised.

Here, the main purpose of setting up a secured credit card is to establish a payment history. The payment history then becomes your credit history. The secured part is to ensure the creditor that you will pay it back, and if not, they already have your money in the account.

Whether a loan or line of credit, the key is to have it with a creditor who reports payments to credit bureaus. Ask them if they report payments before signing up because it is through this reporting that you establish credit.

Note that in the case of the secured credit card, even though the money is deposited up front, interest will be charged if the balance is not paid in full by the statement's due date. Therefore, it is best to spend a little here and there while keeping the amount owed as manageable as possible.

For example, a monthly purchase of $20 that is paid in full every time it comes due will create an excellent payment history. In other words, you don't have to spend a lot to build credit. So, if you don't need it, don't buy it.

Because it is a secured loan or line of credit does not mean it will be cheaper. Generally, new borrowers without a proven credit history (or those with a troubled payment history), will pay higher rates. With this in mind, if you don't stay on top of your payments, the debt can become expensive.

Therefore, the best way to keep your costs down on revolving lines of credit is to pay the full balance owed before the due date.

Every time.

Chapter 4

APPLYING FOR CREDIT

Now that you know the basic types of credit, let's cover some vocabulary as it applies to our topic and go through the process of applying for credit.

It is important to understand the language used in the business. The agreement between a borrower and creditor is serious, so take the time to grasp the following list. Always have a good understanding of what you're signing before putting pen to paper or clicking the online submit button.

Credit Language

Aside from the terms covered previously in chapter 3, there are other words consistent in the lending industry. Before borrowing money, keep the following in mind (list not all-inclusive):

- **Annual percentage rate (APR)** is indicated as a percentage. This is the annual cost to the borrower for the loan amount (interest plus any other fees, such as closing costs, discounts, insurance, etc.);
- **Balance transfer** is moving debt from one credit account to another;
- **Billing cycle** is the number of days between statements issued by the creditor;

» **Co-borrower** is an additional borrower who shares in both the benefit of the funds borrowed as well as the repayment obligation;

» **Compound interest** is the interest on the principal in addition to interest that has accumulated from previous periods;

» **Cosigner** is an additional signer on a loan who agrees to repay the debt if the original borrower defaults;

» **Credit utilization ratio (CUR)** is the percentage of available credit being used between all revolving credit accounts by the borrower;

» **Deferred payment** is when repayment is postponed by creditor;

» **Down payment** is a cash amount paid upfront to the creditor;

» **Grace period** is the time between when the billing cycle ends and when the payment is due, after which late fees, interest, or penalties will be assessed;

» **Interest** is the money the lender makes on the loan;

» **Interest rate** is indicated as a percentage. This is the annual cost (interest portion only) to the borrower for the loan amount;

» **Loan term** is how long the loan is for;

» **Maturity** a/k/a **maturity date** is the date the final payment is due to pay off a loan;

» **Minimum payment due** is the least amount a borrower can pay to stay within the agreement terms and avoid penalties;

» **Origination fee** is the fee charged by the lender for processing the loan;

» **Prepayment penalty** a/k/a **early pay off penalty** is a fee charged for paying a loan off before the due date; and

» **Principal balance** is the unpaid amount of the loan or credit account not including any fees or interest.

Now that we've covered some of the language used when borrowing money, let's move on to the next step.

Looking For A Creditor

Before going crazy with too many options, decide which type of credit you want or need. Start with why you're borrowing money. Next, find a few possible creditors. Research each one and review their credit requirements.

Although you are the borrower, you have the right to ask questions and research potential creditors *before* signing anything.

In most cases, there's no rush to apply for credit. Take your time and make sure the creditor, their products, and their expectations of you, are suitable to your needs.

First, it is important to confirm they are legitimate and reputable. Second (especially when building credit), confirm that they report to the credit bureaus.

Here are a few more things to look for pertaining to the creditor:

» Are they open to new borrowers;

» Do they offer products you might qualify for;

» How long they have been in business;

» Read reviews about them (customer service, availability, etc.);

» What documentation do you need to apply; and

» What is their standing with the Better Business Bureau (BBB).

After finding a couple of creditors that check all the boxes, now research the details pertaining to the type of credit you want. Remember that details will vary and are determined by the creditor on approval.

Here are a few things to consider before applying:

» All conditions & terms;

» Grace period;

» Interest & annual percentage rate; and

» Late fees & penalties.

The Application Process

You know what type of credit you want and have confirmed that you qualify to apply for it. You've completed the research, confirmed that the creditor reports to the bureaus and works with new borrowers. Now let's do a quick overview of the application process.

Whether applying online or in person, certain information will be required to prove your identity.

If applying in person, find out what you need beforehand and take it with you. When applying online, have all documents accessible before beginning the process. And, be honest.

Anticipate providing at least these details:

» Annual income;

» Current employer & employer's address;

» Current home address;

» Date of birth;

» Driver's license number (or equivalent government identification);

» Full name; and

» Social security number (or equivalent).

After completing and submitting the application, the creditor will verify your information and perform a credit check. Depending on where and how you apply, what type of credit you are applying for and how much, this could happen quickly or take a little time.

Credit Check

As mentioned in chapter 1, a potential creditor will conduct a credit check before granting any credit. This will include a thorough review of your credit report, (*see chapters 5 & 6 for more on credit reports*).

Whatever your payment or credit history is, it will likely be revealed on this report. The creditor will review it, compare it to the information on your application, and check other details pertinent to their specific needs and process. If they need more information before making a decision, they will contact you for clarification.

After they have completed their review, you will either be approved or denied. Rejection notices usually list the reasons for being denied. This information should clarify what needs to be improved on your report before moving forward.

Of course, the exciting responses are approvals. Approvals will include the amount you have been approved for, terms, interest, annual percentage rate, and all other details pertaining to your new loan or line of credit.

Congratulations! This is the moment you have been waiting for and you're officially on your way to building credit.

And, in the case of a new credit card, having that piece of plastic for the first time gives a surge of energy and power unlike any other. To rush out to the nearest mall or jump online and load up that shopping cart is tempting.

But wait a minute. Take a few deep breaths and slow down.

Credit is a real responsibility and the debt one acquires when using it in any form comes with real consequences when not repaid.

SUMMARY:
APPLYING FOR CREDIT

Pay attention to these topics before applying for credit:

» Ask questions & gather information

» Common terms & vocabulary used in the credit industry

» Research potential creditors

» Understand creditor's requirements

» Use rejections to make improvements

Chapter 5

CREDIT INQUIRIES

In chapter 4, the creditor conducts a credit check to review a borrower's credit history.

A credit check is a credit inquiry. This inquiry is made by pulling your credit report, or credit file, from one or all three of the major credit bureaus. The three credit bureaus are: Experian™, Equifax®, and TransUnion®.

There are two types of credit inquiries: a hard inquiry and a soft inquiry.

Hard Inquiry

When you apply for credit, you give the creditor permission to request your credit file and review it. When they place their request with the bureau(s), it is called a hard inquiry, or hard pull.

This type of inquiry shows on the credit report as a hit against the credit score and lowers it a bit. When reviewing your report, creditors will see the number of hard inquiries made and when they were requested within the past two years. After two years, an inquiry disappears.

Because hard inquiries can affect your credit score and creditors see them, it is advised not to apply for credit randomly or too frequently.

In fact, if you have been denied credit for a reason that must be fixed, it would be best to address it before applying for credit again. Otherwise, you risk not only another hit against your credit to lower your credit score further, but also another rejection.

Soft Inquiry

After learning about the hard inquiry, you'll be pleased to know the soft inquiry, or soft pull, is less intimidating.

The best thing about a soft inquiry is that it does not impact the credit score. The second best thing is that creditors cannot see it.

Soft inquiries occur when you request a copy of your credit report or when creditors look into a potential borrower's creditworthiness without their knowledge. The latter is done prior to presenting a borrower with a prescreened or preapproved offer.

Prescreened Offers

Prescreened offers are offers to apply for credit. They are generally presented to individuals whose paying habits meet certain criteria set by the creditor.

Such offers are unsolicited and generally come in the mail or via email. Offers vary, depending on the borrower and the creditor. And even though it appears to be a slam dunk, a prescreened or preapproved offer does not guarantee approval.

If you respond to one, a full credit check will be conducted to confirm your details. It will also help the creditor determine if any credit will be extended to you, and if so, how much.

During your review of these offers, you might discover products and options that are better suited to you and your financial goals It could be through one of these opportunities that you obtain a credit card offering updated technology, better reward programs, or a more reasonable APR.

Many times the products being offered are not available to the general public. So, although you might not want them in your mailbox, you may find them educational as to what options are available to you.

New credit lines could help boost your credit utilization ratio and will certainly provide more credit for you to use.

However, it might be wise to wait to apply until your credit score can absorb the ping from the inquiry and is sound enough to provide a positive response from creditors.

SUMMARY:
CREDIT INQUIRIES

Know the differences and importance of credit inquiries:

» Always limit the number & frequency of credit inquiries
» Hard inquiries show on a credit report & affect credit score
» Soft inquiries do not show on report or affect credit score
» Understand prescreened offers & what to expect

Chapter 6

CREDIT REPORTS

Credit reports contain pieces of personal information along with the posted activity of reported accounts. That means that your credit report is the guts and the glory substantiating your payment history. For better or worse, it will probably all be there.

If you're new to the concept of these reports, then take a few minutes to become acquainted. This chapter explores the information found in credit reports, what to look for, and how to inspect them for accuracy.

And, although you might be new to the concept of credit, that does not mean you don't already have a credit file. It's time to find out more.

Credit Report Already Exists

What was that? I have never borrowed money or applied for credit, but there's a credit report in my name? How can that be?

It can happen. And, unless you were expecting it, maybe not for good reasons.

The best way to have a credit file already established and earning you a positive credit history is if a parent, spouse, or other borrower lists you as an authorized user on their account. If the borrower pays responsibly, then this is a fantastic way to start building credit fast.

For example, if a parent takes this course of action for a minor at the age of 15, by the time they are 18, they should have three years of positive payment history under their belt. Of course, if the parent defaults on their payments, then unfortunately, it will be reflected in both credit files.

If this happens, a credit dispute might be necessary to remove the negative information from the minor's file. However, because they are not the primary account holder, the dispute should clear up the matter.

On the other hand, if this is not the situation and you have never applied for credit, there could be an issue if you already have a credit report.

The primary (and possibly only) other reason is identity theft.

If this is the case, then take action immediately. Attention must be paid to not only addressing the identity theft, but also to fixing the true identity owner's credit, (*see chapters 12 & 13 for more on identity theft*).

Now is the time to request your free annual credit report to see if you have one and if so, what is on it.

Ordering & Reviewing A Credit Report

As previously mentioned, there are three major credit bureaus, or credit agencies: Experian™, Equifax®, and TransUnion®.

Everyone is entitled to one free copy of their credit report every twelve months from each of the agencies. You can space them out throughout the year or order one from all three at the same time.

However you choose to do it, at the time of this writing, you can start at AnnualCreditReport.com. Options include ordering online, by phone (allow two weeks for delivery), or in writing (follow their instructions).

Request your credit report today at AnnualCreditReport.com or by calling 1.877.322.8228.

Even though this might be your first credit report, it is good practice to confirm whatever is in your file belongs there and that it is correct. And, although some of the following might not be applicable at this point in your life, keep these items in mind for when they are or could be.

Now, with your credit report in hand, review all information for accuracy, including your name, address and social security number.

Review all addresses listed, past and current, and confirm they are places you have lived. Confirm past and current employment is accurate. In addition, note if there is any reported negative information.

Depending on what the unfavorable item is, there might be limitations as to how long it can remain on your report.

As a general rule, if you find negative entries (including late payments) and they are correct, they will stay in your file for at least seven years.

Following are common negative items found in credit files. Also shown is the time frame each is typically allowed to be posted to a credit report, unless the governing statute of limitations reads otherwise. Always confirm specifics for your situation and the item(s) in question:

» Bankruptcy Filings, 10 years from date of filing;

» Chapter 13 Bankruptcy, 7 years from date of filing;

» Civil Suits, Civil Judgments, Arrest Records, 7 years;

» Collection of Charged Off Accounts, 7 years*;

» Foreclosure, 7 years;

» Paid Tax Lien, 7 years from date paid off; and

» Unpaid Tax Lien, Indefinite (must be paid).

**For these specific types of accounts, note the seven year period begins six months from when you fell behind in payments.*

Next, review all accounts and confirm they are yours. Identify which accounts report to the credit bureaus and which ones do not. Review each account and understand the codes or descriptions as applied, (*see example (a) at end of chapter*).

Reported Accounts

The credit bureau collects the information in your file from companies that report to them. When reviewing the credit file, you will see the reported accounts listed individually with certain financial details pertaining to each specific account, (*see examples (b) and (c) at end of chapter*).

Example:

For example, let's say that you opened a credit card account nine months ago with Bank A. They granted you a credit line of $5,000 and so far, you have made six consecutive monthly payments of $100 each.

The credit report will show the name of Bank A, when the account was opened, the credited line of $5,000, the highest balance ever owed, and the payments. It may also show the outstanding balance owed (if any), at the time of the last reported payment.

While reviewing the payment history, you will notice a few things about your payments.

First, the actual payment amount may or may not be shown.

Second, is timeliness. Payments are either on time or late. Markers for late payments are in thirty day increments, up to 180+ days.

Third, it is common for the most recent payment or two to be missing. If these payments were made within the last three months, don't worry. It can take up to ninety days for reported payments to post.

The only accounts that show on a credit report and include a payment history are those from reporting companies. But that doesn't mean an otherwise non-reporting company won't report nonpayment of an account.

An example of a reporting company that consistently reports your payments is that of a major credit card, such as Bank A. An example of one that generally does not report your good behavior but will report you if the account is turned over to a debt collector or charged off, is the utility company.

Accounts turned over for collection or charged off for nonpayment are damaging to your credit score. And, even if you work hard to amend the situation(s), they could still leave negative marks on your credit report for up to seven years.

Credit Report Discrepancies

In the case of a new borrower, there may not be any reported activity. But as time passes, this will change and when it does, you will want to know what to do in the case of discrepancies.

On that note, review each of the accounts, the financial details, and the account status for accuracy. As previously mentioned, make sure all accounts listed are yours.

> ***Be aware of suspicious activity.***
> ***It might indicate fraud or identity theft.***

On occasion, the timeliness of your payment or the amount you paid might not match what is posted. Likewise, it is possible for the account details to indicate a different payment amount is expected than originally agreed upon.

If any of these occur, address them immediately with the reporting creditor.

Any inaccuracies must be reported to the credit agency that issued the report as well as to the creditor who provided the information. This should be completed in writing (often as a credit dispute letter), and as instructed within the credit report on how to dispute issues.

I know this appears to be overkill. But if there are errors on your report, it is your responsibility to catch them and take the necessary course of action to correct them, (*see chapter 12 for more on credit disputes*).

True Story:

A monthly car payment was indicated to be $487 in the credit file as reported by the dealership at the onset of a loan. However, the borrower's monthly payment statements revealed only $447.

If the borrower makes timely payments of $447 per the statement, they will appear to be underpaying all payments by $40 a month on their loan. Although they are technically doing everything right, this mix-up could lead to a negative credit situation despite their responsible efforts.

In this case, a call to the dealership followed with a letter to the credit bureaus amended the information on the credit report. Thankfully, it was easy to correct and had not yet hurt the borrower's credit.

If you find an error, always start with the creditor who provided the information to the credit agency. In many cases it will be simple to address. Taking this route might also save you a lot of time and energy.

Therefore, knowing mistakes happen is another reason to check your credit report for accuracy.

Additionally and as time passes, accounts will be closed by either you or a creditor. And credit reports do reveal when accounts were closed and by whom.

Open accounts that are supposed to be closed should be updated on the report. If you find any, send written notification to the creditor and request that they notify the bureau. To confirm the correct action is taken, write your own letter to the credit bureau and include the necessary details.

When *you* have chosen to close an account, include this in your letter to both the creditor as well as the credit bureau.

Example (a): Sample Credit File Labels and Account Descriptions

Account Column Title Descriptions:		
Acct Number:	The Account Number Reported by Credit Grantor	
Date Acct Opened:	The Date that the Credit Grantor Opened the Account	
High Credit:	The Highest Amount Charged	
Credit Limit:	The Highest Amount Permitted	
Terms Duration:	The Number of Installments or Payments	
Terms Frequency:	The Scheduled Time Between Payments	
Months Reviewed:	The Number of Months Reviewed	
Activity Designator:	The Most Recent Account Activity	
Creditor Class:	The Type of Company Reporting the Account	
Date Rptd:	Date of Last Reported Update	
Balance Amt:	The Total Amount Owed as of the Date Reported	
Status:	Condition of Account When Last Updated by Creditor	
Amt Past Due:	The Amount Past Due as of the Date Reported	
Date of Last Payment:	The Date of Last Payment	
Actual Pay Amt:	The Actual Amount of Last Payment	
Sched Pay Amt:	The Requested Amount of Last Payment	
Date of 1st Delinquency:	The Date of 1st Delinquency	
Date of Last Activity:	The Date of the Last Account Activity	
Date Maj Delq Rptd:	The Date the 1st Major Delinquency was Reported	
Charge Off Amt:	The Amount Charged Off by Creditor	
Deferred Pay Date:	The 1st Payment Due Date for Deferred Loans	
Balloon Pay Amt:	The Amount of Final (Balloon) Payment	
Balloon Pay Date:	The Date of Final (Balloon) Payment	
Account History Status Code Descriptions:		
1: 30–59 Days Past Due	5: 150–179 Days Past Due	J: Voluntary Surrender
2: 60–89 Days Past Due	6: 180 or More Days Past Due	K: Repossession
3: 90–119 Days Past Due	G: Collection Account	L: Charge Off
4: 120–149 Days Past Due	H: Foreclosure	

Example (b): Sample Account Details on Credit Report

$36 ÷ $3,000 = 1%

Reported Balance | Credit Limit | Credit Utilization

0% 10% 20% 30% 40% 50% 60% 70% 80% 90% 100%

Details Payments

Overview

Account Number	XXXXXXXXXXXX XX XX	**Months Reviewed**	39
Account Status	PAYS_AS_AGREED	**Activity Designator**	
Owner	INDIVIDUAL	**Terms Frequency**	MONTHLY
Account Type	REVOLVING	**Term Duration**	
Creditor Classification		**Purchased From**	
Loan Type	CREDIT_CARD	**Sold To**	
Original Creditor Name			

Balance and Amounts

Balance	$36
Credit Limit	$3,000
High Credit	$2,274
Available Credit	$2,964

Account Dates

Date Opened	Mar 02, 2018
Date Reported	Jun 30, 2021
Date of Last Activity	Jun 01, 2021
Date of First Delinquency	

This is a portion of an online credit report, or credit file, provided by a credit bureau. At the top is the CUR with the percentage scale, following is an overview of the account details.

Example (c): Sample Account Payment History & Details on Credit Report

$36 ÷ $3,000 = 1%

Reported Balance · Credit Limit · Credit Utilization

0% 10% 20% 30% 40% 50% 60% 70% 80% 90% 100%

Details | **Payments**

Payment History

View up to 7 years of monthly payment history on this account. The numbers indicated in each month represent the number of days a payment was past due; the letters indicate other account events, such as bankruptcy or collections.

	Jan	Feb	Mar	Apr	May	Jun	Jul	Aug	Sep	Oct	Nov	Dec
2021	OK	OK	OK	OK	OK							
2020	OK	OK	OK	OK	OK	OK	OK	OK	OK	OK	OK	OK
2019	OK	OK	OK	OK	OK	OK	OK	OK	OK	OK	OK	OK
2018			OK	OK	OK	OK	OK	OK	OK	OK	OK	OK

OK Pays as Agreed · Too New to Rate · Past Due · B Bankruptcy · C Collection Account · R Repossession · CO Charge Off · No Data Available

Payment Details

Months Reviewed	39	**Date of Last Payment**	Jun 01, 2021
Payment Responsibility	INDIVIDUAL	**Scheduled Payment Amount**	$25
Deferred Payment Start Date		**Actual Payment Amount**	
Date Closed		**Charge Off Amount**	

Other Payments & Delinquencies

Balloon Payment Date		**Delinquency First Reported**	
Balloon Payment Amount		**Amount Past Due**	

Reviewing the same account on the credit report as seen in example (b), this image reveals the payment history and details as presented by the credit bureau in this online credit file.

SUMMARY:
CREDIT REPORTS

Keep track of your credit report & the details:

» Always correct errors immediately

» Order credit report & monitor annually

» Research & report suspicious activity immediately

» Review thoroughly: accounts, accuracy & activity

Chapter 7

PRE-APPLICATION PREP

You have decided to apply for credit and have something in mind for how to use it. You're equipped with your credit file and have reviewed it for accuracy. Everything lines up.

But, really what difference does any of this make and how do creditors use the information found in a report? And, what can you do to make sure your application will be approved?

Before you whip out a few applications, let's take a closer look at the details and try to see things through a potential creditor's eyes.

Do Account Status & Details Matter?

That's a great question. To many they would seem irrelevant. To creditors, they indicate more than just your borrowing interests and habits.

And yes, if you're a new borrower without any credit history, this information may not yet apply to you. However, it is included because it helps in understanding how potential creditors interpret what they see on a report when deciding whether or not to extend credit to a borrower.

On a side note, two examples of positive debt are student loans and mortgages because both are considered to be assets. In most cases, whatever we purchase will depreciate in value, which makes it a negative debt.

Okay, back to the potential creditor.

When a creditor considers lending money, they look at several things. These will include at least: your income, any alimony you receive, how much money you owe, how long your loans are scheduled for, your payment history on existing accounts, how long you have had the accounts, your credit utilization ratio, and how much potential debt you can incur immediately.

Added together, this information indicates the level of credit risk you pose as a client. A quick look at existing debt opportunities can reveal a lot, even without examining details such as income and payment history.

Example:

You have a student loan, a major credit card (MJ CC), and a department store credit card (DS CC).

Your student loan is for $25,000, the credit line on MJ CC is $10,000 and DS CC has a line of $2,000.

When a lender looks at this and adds everything up, they see a potential immediate debt possibility of $12,000 on top of the student loan. Because these accounts are already open, you have access to that money.

At any moment, you could go on a shopping spree and rack up $12,000 of negative debt. And although your student loan is considered positive debt, it is still money you owe.

On another note, they could also consider the $12,000 as part of your credit utilization ratio, *(see chapter 11 for more on CUR)*.

Pertaining to closed accounts, if an account was closed by you, then it was your decision to wrap it up. An example where you might close a line of credit could be a credit card opened for a discount when purchasing furniture that you have since paid off.

If, however, the account was closed by the creditor, then there is the possibility of issues with the borrower. With certain exceptions, accounts closed by creditors often indicate red flags to new potential lenders.

Two exceptions would be a mortgage or auto loan being paid off. When the debt is repaid for either of these loans, the lender will close the account. And because the payment history will be revealed to potential lenders, you should confirm that the story it tells is accurate.

While building credit, you won't want to close accounts. Eventually though, you will find it beneficial when a line of credit no longer serves you. Keeping your credit file tidy with current, useful accounts is a good idea and allows room in the debt-to-income ratio when applying for a new loan or line of credit.

The more you do voluntarily to show financial responsibility, the more appealing you will be to potential lenders. But don't be too hasty to clear out the clutter, (*see chapter 11 for more on closing accounts*).

Consider all details before closing an account.

Prepare Before Applying

For a borrower without any credit history, there is not much you can do to prepare your credit before applying. However, regardless of your status, make sure you are as prepared as possible for the highest chance of getting approved.

Go ahead and revisit chapter 4 to brush up on the information there. Make sure to complete your research and have all of your documentation in order.

If you are a new borrower without a credit history but with a payment history, request letters from those to whom you have made regular payments. Examples here could include utility companies, landlords, or maybe a neighbor you bought a car from and paid off with monthly payments. The more structured the entity (business vs. individual), the better.

Plan ahead before applying. Allow enough time to ask for the letter(s) and receive something back in writing. With the exception of the neighbor, ask them to report to the credit bureaus. It can't hurt to ask, and it's possible that they will.

Regardless, in the case of an in-person application, such as at a bank or credit union, these letters could be useful. Take copies with you for the creditor's review when considering your application.

Likewise, in the case of an online application, if you can upload documents, you should include them there. Any proof that you are and have been financially responsible is better than none at all.

For all borrowers, begin with a review of your credit report. The best way to approach borrowing money is to know what lenders will find in your credit history before you apply. This advantage allows you to get a jump on resolving issues.

Start the process early to address potential issues prior to requesting the loan or line of credit. The minimum of three months is suggested because items reported on credit files may be up to ninety days behind. If you want to make improvements for new creditors to see, you need to allow for this delay in posting.

Naturally, if you need more time to make the corrections and can afford to wait, then postpone applying until the time is right.

Collectively, this foresight and preparation could pave the way for a path of less resistance when you complete your application.

Let's refer to the previous example again, but now let's get ready to ask for more credit.

You want to buy a car within the next few months. Reviewing your options, you decide $10,000 should be enough.

Using only the information provided in the example, adding another ten grand to your debt is a substantial increase. If your credit history is perfect and has been established for at least a year, you might fare well.

But even so, this is not taking into consideration any living expenses. And if you live with your parents or someone else who pays for everything, you are in better shape than the average borrower.

No matter your overall expenses, you might want to tighten things up a bit before approaching a creditor.

Keep in mind that whether or not your credit accounts are maxed out is not the point. The money is available and the possibility to exhaust it exists. Therefore, creditors might consider these totals even if you do not owe it in full when you submit the application.

Remember, one of the key factors when applying for credit is your income. If your annual income before taxes is $30,000, and you have a student loan for $25,000 plus the existing $12,000 immediately available through credit cards, do you think you can afford another loan?

Many creditors will see this situation as high risk, and probably deny the credit. Some may be willing, but often with high interest rates, fees, and over-the-top payments.

In fact, if you have time, stop in and ask a few questions of the potential creditor before submitting an application. You may get a better feel for how to proceed based on their requirements.

Regardless, try to avoid applying until you have done everything you can to ensure approval. Keep in mind that every application results in a credit check and that creates a hit against your credit. And you definitely do not want to be racking up unnecessary credit inquiries.

Squeeze Here For More Credit

Alright, we have the current example as your situation and you want to borrow $10,000 for the car. Without quitting school to try to cancel the loan, how can you increase your odds of approval?

First, consider getting a job or additional source of income. Second, pay off all balances on the credit cards as soon as possible and keep them that way, especially until you get the loan.

Even though creditors will still see the credit line as possible debt, it will work in your favor to have less outstanding debt. Plus, paying them off in full is always best practice.

But I know those options might be impossible if you're already working and going to school. Life is expensive, and sometimes paying credit card balances in full is too much of a reach.

I get it. Remember, I've been there.

So, in times like this, I applied option number three. This strategy has helped me in the past to squeeze out more credit, and there is always the chance it can help you, too.

Let's see what you have to work with when looking at your current debt situation.

Unless you can work magic on the student loan, that is probably what it will be. Of course, periodically research your loan situation for updates.

Next, look at the two revolving lines of credit. These are referred to as negative debt and, unless they help with your credit utilization ratio, are the first place to make adjustments.

The first account, MJ CC, has a credit line of $10,000. This account has been open for eight months. Your highest balance to date was $2,000, and you currently owe $300.

The second account, DS CC, has a credit line of $2,000 and has been open for a year. You use it here and there for minor purchases. Your highest balance to date has been $250, and you currently owe $50.

As you can see, you have more credit available on each of these accounts than you are using. And although this is great, I would start tweaking here.

When you need to apply for more credit but do not have an increase in income, adjusting existing credit lines is the perfect place to begin.

Note that you do not have to close accounts, nor do you have to stop using them. In fact, while building credit, I would not suggest either of these actions.

However, you can request a reduction in credit lines to make room for more credit to be available to you. Of course, you don't want to jeopardize yourself in the case of emergencies, but if a true emergency were to arise, creditors have been known to work with responsible borrowers.

Looking at both accounts, I see that MJ CC could easily be reduced to a credit line of $4,000 and DS CC to $500. These two adjustments will clear up $7,500 worth of available credit while leaving plenty to use.

Now when a creditor looks at your report (providing it has had time to reflect these changes), they will see your potential debt above the student loan to be $4,500. What a difference that will make, from the previous $12,000!

And assuming the loan for $10,000 is approved, you would only be adding (without interest and fees), $2,500 to your potential debt. But with that, you also have a new car, (*see example (d) on following page*).

Note that these changes can only be made if current balances on the accounts are lower than the new credit line request. If the balances are too high, then keep this strategy in mind for future use.

But if everything is in line and this option makes sense for your needs, reach out to your creditors and place the requests.

If you initiate with a phone call, follow up with the details in writing. And always keep a copy of all communication pertaining to your accounts for your records.

Example (d): Hypothetical Accounts & Adjustments

Account Creditor	**Credit Line**
DS CC	$2,000
MJ CC	$10,000
Student Loan	$25,000
Potential Debt	**$37,000**
After Suggested Strategy	
DS CC	$500
MJ CC	$4,000
Student Loan	$25,000
Adjusted Potential Debt	**$29,500**
After Suggested Strategy With New Car Loan	
DS CC	$500
MJ CC	$4,000
New Car Loan	$10,000
Student Loan	$25,000
New Potential Debt	**$39,500**

SUMMARY:
PRE-APPLICATION PREP

Do your prep work before applying for credit:

» Always review credit report a few months before applying

» Confirm all details are correct on report

» Fix negative items before applying, if possible

» Maintain all accounts for good standing

» Reduce credit lines if necessary to increase credit availability

Chapter 8

INTEREST & APR

Understanding the details of a financial agreement is paramount to making sound decisions. When it comes to borrowing money, either through a loan or line of credit, it's helpful to have a grasp on these two terms: interest rate and annual percentage rate (APR).

Again, for the purpose of this guide, all references will pertain to credit and the act of borrowing.

Interest Rate & Annual Percentage Rate (APR)

The interest rate of a loan or credit account is indicated as a percentage and that percentage is based on the amount of money borrowed, also referred to as the principal. The interest is the profit the lender keeps for letting someone use their money.

The annual percentage rate is the cost of loan to the borrower. Also indicated as a percentage, this number includes the interest plus any fees associated with the loan. Examples of these additional costs include closing costs, broker fees, points, and more, depending on the type of loan.

When applying for a loan, it is important to consider and compare which option best suits your needs. Using the APR, you can compare total loan costs. For example, you might compare a loan that is interest only to one with a lower interest rate that also has points.

This can be complicated if you don't know what you're doing. But if you do some research, you can remove a lot of the guesswork.

An excellent tool for this is a free online calculator. Find the right one for what you want to know and simply plug in your loan details to see the actual numbers. By exploring options and using these types of resources, you will be able to make educated decisions.

Again, there are many details and variations to consider per situation and borrower. It is up to each individual to understand their needs and do their homework before signing an agreement.

Understand interest and annual percentage rates when applying for credit.

Now let's look at two common types of interest rates available for loans.

Fixed & Variable Interest Rates

When a borrower takes out a loan or mortgage, the interest rate is attached to the amount borrowed. The type of loan they have determines how their payment will be applied to the interest and principal balance as the loan is paid back.

All payments are structured to include a portion for the principal and a portion for interest.

If the loan is a fixed-rate loan, the interest rate will remain the same for the duration of the loan. Payments will be determined at a set amount that will not vary until possibly the last payment. However, the application of the funds from the payment itself will shift as the loan is paid down.

At the beginning, the bulk of the payment will go toward paying interest with a small portion applied to the principal balance. As time passes and the interest portion of the loan is being reduced, then a larger portion of the payment will be applied to the principal.

The fixed-rate loan is predictable and relatively straightforward. On the other hand, the variable-rate loan is a bit trickier.

Having a variable rate indicates the interest being charged can and will fluctuate with the market or an index, such as the prime rate. These loans are also referred to as having a floating interest rate. This fluctuation, or floating, is what makes it variable.

The attraction to a variable-rate loan is that payments will be lower while the index is low. However, as the index used for the loan increases, so will the payment. This feature often takes borrowers by surprise when their payments become higher than expected.

If you dabble here, be careful. Understand when it makes sense to use this option and when it doesn't. Research the pros and cons based on your situation and always pay attention to avoid unpleasant surprises.

Lowering High Rates

Credit card rates are generally the highest you will see between all of your borrowing options. While it is common for loans to be set up with a single-digit interest rate or APR, credit card accounts will almost always be in the double digits.

Traditionally, new borrowers have been charged higher rates along with those who have a low credit score or troubled payment history. Borrowers in these categories are considered to be high risk for the lender. Therefore, they are charged more to borrow money until they become established.

It is common for new borrowers and those who have a poor payment history to have rates in the twenties and possibly higher (all details creating variations). However, if payments have been made regularly and on time for at least a year, then ask the creditor if they will lower the APR on the account.

For example, when a credit card's APR at 29.99% is lowered to 21.99%, it doesn't look like much has happened. But this could save the borrower a lot of money if they miss a due date or have to carry a balance.

Every creditor is different and not all will honor the request. And, although this concept might apply to loans, receiving an APR reduction is most applicable to credit cards.

But as Mom says, it never hurts to ask.

Pertaining to credit cards and carrying a balance, lowering the APR whenever possible is an excellent proactive move toward saving money. Always do what you can today to be in a better position tomorrow.

With countless unknowns in our futures, you never know when you will need the credit, and there could be a time when it is not possible to pay the entire balance in full.

Which leads to another word of caution.

When a lower APR is granted, do not use it as an excuse to carry a balance or create unnecessary debt. Even at a lower APR, debt becomes expensive and can quickly spiral out of control.

Zero Percent Offers

While providing words of caution, here is one for low or zero-percent offers.

These offers can be attached to a variety of products, including (list not all-inclusive):

» An introductory period for new credit card;

» Appliance purchases;

» Auto loans;

» Balance transfers; and

» Furniture purchases.

As tempting as they are, these little beauties come with fine print that packs a punch. Although it is always recommended to read the fine print before signing anything, please do exercise this suggestion for any and all such offers.

Again, details will vary. However, there are a few things to consider with these amazing deals and they include:

» Advertised APR is for qualified borrowers;

» Advertised APR is for a set time & will expire;

» Any missed or late payment may cancel the low/zero APR;

» Late or missed payment may cause interest to be charged retroactive to original purchase amount & date (can be costly);

» New APR after expiration of the advertised APR will be higher; and

» Potential for steep penalties & fees.

In summary, unless your newly favorite uncle is giving you the money to fulfill your dreams, you will be charged something to borrow funds.

Take time to read and understand what the costs will be to you. Don't be afraid to ask the creditor questions and take notes of their responses.

And, even though it sounds like an unnecessary, out-of-date process, start and maintain a file about the account and keep your notes there. You never know when you'll need to clarify or confirm a detail.

SUMMARY:
INTEREST & APR

Understand the costs of interest and APR and keep track:

» Always review all details before signing anything

» Be careful with variable interest rates

» Request lower interest & APR

» Understand interest vs. APR

» Use caution with low or zero interest/APR loans or deals

Chapter 9

BUDGETING & PAYMENTS

Admittedly, budgeting is never on the fun-things-to-do list. However, it is crucial to the success of establishing and maintaining financial stability.

Why Should I Budget?

Understanding your financial obligations is necessary. How much money is coming in and how much is going out (and where it is going), are all revealed when a budget is created. Having this information available to review and examine every week can influence your purchasing decisions.

To stay on top of things, I suggest putting together a tracker for your reference. It should track all expenses: monthly, semi-annual, and annual. Include your income (after taxes).

It's important to be honest and log everything, including all minor purchases. Remember, this is for your benefit and when used correctly, it will help you structure your finances for complete, timely payments.

Careful scrutiny of your expenses will reveal where to make changes, if possible. And while reviewing them, your tracker will expose when your finances will be under the most stress. This tidbit allows for you to plan ahead and prepare your finances for the heavier months.

A practical scenario is having two dentist appointments a year for routine cleanings. Without dental insurance, they are both semi-annual, out-of-pocket expenses. Where these appointments fall in the calendar will make for more expensive months. If excluded from your budget sheet, those two months' expenses might bring unpleasant surprises.

Example:

Recently, I reviewed my expenses and realized I could shift a few things to make my life easier. This makes for a great example, so here it is, (*see example (e) at end of chapter for table format*).

I pay my auto insurance twice a year, my homeowner's insurance once a year and property taxes once a year.

Additionally, I visit the dentist and dermatologist twice a year and neither are covered by health insurance. Therefore, they are both semi-annual, out-of-pocket expenses to me. Prior to making any changes, four of these were scheduled to happen in May and the other four six months later, in November.

The home insurance, auto insurance, and property taxes are not easy to move, so they will remain. The unmovable breakdown is: one auto insurance payment plus the home insurance in May, the other auto insurance payment and property taxes in November.

However, the dermatologist and dentist appointments are movable.

After reviewing everything but wanting to stay timely with my appointments, I shifted both of these to one month later. Now, they are scheduled for June and December.

Although the shift is only one month for the appointment dates, it makes a difference in the amount of money going out per month. And, if I pay for the appointments with a credit card, I gain an additional thirty days to pay. This strategy technically stretches out the time between having to shell out the payment to a possible sixty days.

Here it is with hypothetical amounts to help you visualize this strategy:

» Auto insurance, $1,000, twice per year;

» Dental cleaning, $150, twice per year;

» Dermatologist, $250, twice per year;

» Home insurance, $2,000, once per year; and

» Property taxes, $4,000, once per year.

Before moving the appointments, the monthly expenses for only these items (excluding all other expenses) are as follows:

» $3,400 for May; and

» $5,400 for November.

After moving each semi-annual appointment one month later to June and December, here are the new amounts (excluding all other expenses):

» $3,000 for May;

» $400 for June;

» $5,000 for November; and

» $400 for December.

On the surface, shifting the $400 might not appear to be helpful. Compared to the larger sums that remain for May and November, it doesn't look like much. But, when you add in all other expenses, that $400 could be the determining factor in whether or not other bills are manageable.

This is a simple example. But the idea is to understand when and how to apply this strategy, and then do it.

Before creating unhealthy financial habits, consider implementing a sound practice. Now is the time to grasp the concept of budgeting and begin applying it daily to build your credit as solidly as possible.

Tightening up and refining your budget is an ongoing process. Start by reviewing your shopping and spending habits. When you look over your tracker and credit card statements, ask yourself if the purchases are needs or wants.

Also consider this question when grocery shopping, reviewing entertainment expenses, and other miscellaneous purchases (many of which prove to be unnecessary).

Again, you must be honest for this process to be helpful and worth your time and effort.

Account Analysis

Take the time to review what you owe every month for each account. Look at the minimum amount due to maintain steady, timely payments. By now, you know it is best practice to pay the entire balance in full every month on a credit card. But there will be times when that won't be possible.

Regardless, it is imperative when building credit to create and maintain consistency with reported payments. Making regular, timely payments is necessary, even if paying less than the required minimum due. In the case of a tight financial squeeze, what else can you do?

Completing an account analysis and applying a creative approach might be necessary to get you through. This is not to say that unreported accounts can be ignored or pushed to the back burner. For example, utility companies seldom report, but can you afford to have your power shut off?

Me neither.

Therefore, know that all accounts are equally important. However, if things are tight, some accounts take priority when figuring out the amounts to be paid until the full balance can be addressed without going hungry. Consider the following when in this situation.

First, is interest being charged? If so, how much? Make a note next to each account if interest is accruing and at what percentage. Also track the minimum payment required and the outstanding balance.

If it is a loan, note if there is a penalty for paying it down before it comes due. If so, then such an account should receive only the payment required to prevent additional penalties.

Top Priority Accounts

Now that you know which account balances are accruing interest and at what rate, you can determine which ones become top priority.

Top priority, again, does not mean ignoring other debt. It simply means those accounts require more attention first when times get tough.

What kind of attention? Great question!

Start with the basics. If you have two major credit cards with a balance, one at 22% APR and the other with 15% APR, then you can see the first one will cost you more whenever you carry a balance.

Assuming neither credit line is maxed out, remove the card with the higher rate from your wallet. Lock it up in a safe, but out-of-sight place.

Do not add to this card's balance (online or off), but rather focus on paying it off. Only when necessary, use the card with the lower APR for new purchases.

Accounts with the highest rate will cost the most every month. These are the accounts you want to pay above the minimum due as frequently as possible.

At the beginning, this might sound daunting. But as you adjust your spending habits and money allocation, you will see it start to work.

To help consumers understand their potential financial obligations, the government requires creditors to provide additional account details. These changes now require all credit card statements show the outstanding balance, amount due, how much you will pay if only the minimum due is paid, and how long it will take, (*see example (f) at end of chapter*).

Take a moment to review your statement and familiarize yourself with how much the current debt could cost. Now, keep those larger numbers in mind every time you pull out a credit card for a frivolous purchase.

Can you, in truth, really afford what it will eventually cost you?

If you don't really need it, do yourself a favor and leave it at the store. For larger purchases in particular, sleep on it for a few nights and see if you can live without it. You might be surprised at how easy it is to walk away from making pointless purchases, and how rewarding it will be.

Now that your top-priority expenses have been determined based on level of importance first and amount of interest being charged, you can—and absolutely should—begin structuring a monthly budget plan.

Banker's Tip:

Before making a payment on a credit card, allow creditors to process the statement. This ensures the amount owed is posted to your credit file first, followed by your timely payment.

And for the sake of building credit, this is especially important when paying the balance in full.

Example (e): Hypothetical Expenses And Frequency*

Expense	Frequency	Due	Amount
Auto Insurance	2 x year	May/Nov	$1,000
Dental Cleaning	2 x year	May/Nov	$150
Dermatologist	2 x year	May/Nov	$250
Home Insurance	1 x year	May	$2,000
Property Taxes	1 x year	November	$4,000
May			**$3,400**
November			**$5,400**
After Suggested Strategy			
Auto Insurance	2 x year	May/Nov	$1,000
Dental Cleaning	2 x year	June/Dec	$150
Dermatologist	2 x year	June/Dec	$250
Home Insurance	1 x year	May	$2,000
Property Taxes	1 x year	November	$4,000
May			**$3,000**
June			**$400**
November			**$5,000**
December			**$400**

**All other potential monthly expenses excluded and not shown here.*

Example (f): Actual Credit Card Payment Information From Creditor*

PAYMENT INFORMATION

New Balance $7,851.00

Minimum Payment Due 158.00

Payment Due Date May 8, 2016

Late Payment Warning: If we do not receive your minimum payment by the date listed above, you may have to pay a late fee up to $35.00 and your purchase and balance transfer APRs for new transactions may be increased up to the Penalty APR of 18.99% variable.

Minimum Payment Warning: If you make only the minimum payment each period, you will pay more in interest and it will take you longer to pay off your balance. For example:

If you make no additional charges using this card and each month you pay...	You will pay off the balance shown on this statement in about...	And you will end up paying an estimated total of...
Only the minimum	20 years	$15,909
$261	3 years	$9,394 (Savings = $6,515)

**This is actual payment information from a creditor. Notice the portion in the shaded boxes and the figures below them. If only the minimum payment is paid per month, then it will take 20 years to pay off an original balance of $7,851. If all minimum payments are made on time, the interest charged is a whopping $8,058, making the total paid $15,909!*

Note the Late Payment Warning details.
If at any time a payment is late, then the APR could rise in addition to fees applied for late payments.

This example should be enough to scare anyone into paying down a debt as quickly as possible, rather than relying on the simplicity of only making a minimum payment.

Just think of what you could do with an extra $8,058 in your pocket ... and this is only from one credit card!

Get your mindset in gear to build a solid foundation for your credit and financial future.

Track your daily spending every month for a year. Notice where the money is going and eliminate unnecessary purchases.

Think smart before spending money.

Realize that every dime counts and consider every purchase carefully. Fine tune your spending habits and understand that even though it goes on a piece of plastic when you buy it, you will eventually have to pay for it.

If you do not have the cash to pay for it, assume you can't afford it until you have the money in the account.

This is not the same as believing you are broke and can't afford things in general. It's a way to set yourself up for a stronger financial future.

Also, if you must use a debit card, only use it where you will not incur fees.

Examine your finances to discover where you can make changes and apply them for greater savings and less pointless spending.

A positive mindset to maintain while building your credit (and possibly beyond), is to live beneath your means.

This is not a negative attitude toward money.
The concept is to keep you on track when you are tempted to spend.

Learn to live with less fluff.
When it comes to your finances, you'll be glad you did!

SUMMARY:
BUDGETING & PAYMENTS

Master the art of budgeting. Be sure to include these tips:

» Be honest with yourself about your spending habits

» Create tracker of all expenses: monthly, semi-annual & annual

» Include all income & purchases: cash, credit & debit

» Live beneath your means

» Make all payments on time

» Review where money is going; make necessary cutbacks

Chapter 10

GET STARTED

We've covered a lot of ground at this point and there is always more to learn. Credit is an ever-growing topic, but by now, you know enough to start building credit.

Note that depending on where you are in life could determine where to begin. Feel free to pick and choose from here to suit your needs because it's impossible for this to be a one-size-fits-all approach.

Do your best to be prepared before approaching potential creditors. Review the information in this chapter, revisit chapters 3, 4, and 7, and then get started.

Remember that every time you submit an application, a hard inquiry will be posted against your credit. Randomly applying to numerous places in hopes of approval often backfires.

Keep it simple and keep your requests within reason by only borrowing what you need while getting started.

Student Loans

Going to college can be a life-altering opportunity. Many colleges offer financial programs to attend. Some students will qualify for grants and scholarships, which alleviate much of the financial stress. However, for those who don't qualify, they can apply for student loans.

Check with the school and your bank for loan options and applicable rates. Make sure you understand when the loan repayment process is expected to begin and the costs involved.

Next, check with the federal government and research their direct loans and available rates. In many cases, a direct loan from the government will be the most economical and attractive route.

At the time of this writing, there are three direct loans available from the government. Each has its own requirements and targeted audience:

» Direct subsidized loans;

» Direct unsubsidized loans; and

» Direct PLUS loans.

While reviewing the requirements and learning which type of loan is appropriate for you, check out the benefits that come with it. Although your research should reveal more than included here, the following details stand out.

The most notable of the benefits is that these loans generally come with low, fixed interest rates and are structured with repayment plans based on the borrower's income. Additionally, repayment is expected to begin six months after you leave school or your enrollment drops below half-time.

This last detail is worth focusing on because other loan options might require earlier repayment. Going to school and passing classes presents enough challenges. Therefore, without abusing the system, take every benefit you can and use it to your advantage.

Personal Loans

In general, I would not suggest taking out a personal loan without a purpose in mind, like making a purchase, unless you are experienced in how else to use the money. But that is another topic.

However, when first starting to build credit, this might be a good option to exercise. If you don't need the money and are asking for the loan solely to build credit, then request a small amount.

Keep in mind that the bank or credit union might require a cosigner or for the loan to be secured. If secured, this will also determine how much will be approved.

Secured or unsecured, if the creditor approves a loan for $500 or $1,000, that is perfect. That's not too much to be overwhelming or too dangerous if you do spend it all.

Regardless of the amount you qualify for, always review the details. Use this as practice for all future financial transactions and confirm the interest and APR, repayment structure, payment amounts, and if there is a penalty for early pay off.

If you are borrowing the money strictly to establish credit, put it in an account where it will earn some interest but not penalize you for withdrawals. Then, when you need to make a payment, draw from that account.

Yes, if you use the entire term to pay off the loan, it will cost you something to have borrowed the funds. But in the meantime, assuming you make every payment on time, you're building credit.

Auto Loans

Auto loans can be tricky. If you need to buy a car and must finance it, research the difference between obtaining an auto loan from the dealership versus a personal loan. Depending on which option is the most desirable, go from there. Note that a cosigner may be required.

When buying a vehicle, you'll want to anticipate possible surprises. A few things are noted here, but always ask questions and confirm details before agreeing to the lender's terms.

One thing to expect is to have to carry full coverage on the vehicle until it's paid off, unless otherwise stated. When you have a vehicle in mind, call the insurance company for the quote.

Another is high interest rates. If this is your first loan, expect double digits. Be thrilled if you qualify for anything less than that.

There will be additional expenses such as tax, title, and other fees. Warranties and insurance policies will most likely be offered and strongly suggested.

And, of course, how much money will you need to put down?

The more cash you have to put down, the better your chances of being approved and at a lower APR, although this is not a guarantee. Remember, creditors take several factors into consideration prior to approving a loan and determining the terms.

An auto loan is a secured loan. If you take one out, honor each and every payment.

Late or missed payments put you on the road to trouble. If you know you cannot make a payment, try to work something out with the lender before you are late. When you miss the mark, contact them immediately to discuss available options.

Delinquent or missed payments place your vehicle at risk for being repossessed. As if losing your ride isn't tough enough, the details will also be posted to your credit file, creating a blemish that will be hard to fix.

Department Store Credit Cards

As mentioned previously, department store credit cards are usually accepted only at that store. But don't rule them out as a great way to start building credit.

Many people beginning their credit adventure reside with their parents or spouse. In either case, if this is you, your needs may be being taken care of by whomever you live with. If so, you probably don't need a credit card that is accepted everywhere. Not yet, anyway.

Department store credit lines tend to be lower and easier to acquire. However, that doesn't make them free or insignificant. In fact, the APR is generally high. And because they usually report to the credit agencies, they must be taken seriously.

If you start here and are accepted, use it modestly and maintain only one department store card. Remember, creditors will look for various forms of credit on your credit report, so consider a small loan if you need more.

Starter Credit Cards

The starter credit card is an exciting option for anyone looking to build credit. This includes international students, individuals without credit, those with minimal credit, and those with a poor credit history.

There are a variety of starter cards to choose from, each one offering its own set of desirable options. Here are some possible goodies to look for when considering which card will best suit you (list not all-inclusive):

» Cash back on purchases;

» Consideration for higher credit line;

» First late payment fee forgiveness;

» Free FICO credit score on statement;

» No annual fee;

» No credit history required;

» No foreign transaction fee;

» No penalty APR; and

» Travel perks.

These credit cards are offered by major companies and are an excellent place to launch your credit future. Examine the pros and cons to determine which card will best complement your typical spending needs and lifestyle.

Carefully review all details before submitting an application. Confirm all fees, penalties, and expirations of special offers.

Major Credit Cards

Granted the department store credit card is limited. The starter credit card should be able to meet your needs and again, is offered by most major players.

However, if you believe the starter card is not your best option yet still want to aim higher and have a card widely accepted by gas stations, grocery stores, restaurants, retailers and utility companies, then be my guest.

Major credit cards make the world accessible.

Literally. So, be careful.

If you don't have any credit and choose not to pursue a starter card, then a secured credit card will probably be required. Start with a modest line of $300 and go from there.

Although it doesn't sound like much, $300 will allow you to buy things and go places, while keeping your account manageable. And, like the personal loan of less than $1,000, it will help you establish credit without getting into an overwhelming financial predicament.

Using a credit card is ridiculously easy today and that means getting in over your head is, too.

To benefit from the use of credit cards, one must be financially responsible. If your current financial situation can handle an additional $50 a month in frivolous expense without causing a pinch on something such as paying your rent, then that is all you should spend.

However, buying something for the sole purpose of using the credit card can lead to poor shopping habits and a closet full of clutter.

Remember, what you buy today on credit must be paid for with real money. And if you cannot make the payment in full before the due date, you will be charged interest.

Interest will accrue daily until that amount is paid off. As you charge other purchases on top of that initial amount, you will be paying more on top of more.

Therefore, rather than making frivolous purchases to build credit, why not use that gorgeous new credit line for something you already pay for?

Example:

An excellent way to build credit with a major credit card is to use it only for one or two bills, such as cable and phone. These should have been accounted for in your monthly expenses, so they are not additional expenses creating additional stress.

Also, neither the cable nor phone company report to credit bureaus. However, by paying these two bills with the credit card and then paying the credit card balance in full every month, you will have accomplished three things at the same time. These are:

» Avoiding frivolous purchases & wasting money;

» Keeping your monthly bills current; and

» Successfully establishing excellent credit!

In most cases, the cable and phone accounts can be set up for automatic payment. If this suits you, confirm your credit line will support it before setting it up. Always stay on top of not only the amounts being charged, but also the charges being posted to your credit card.

In the case of a $300 credit line, if you have a $50 cable bill every month and your phone varies, say between $75–$100, then you must ensure that at least $150 of the credit line is always available for those two automatic charges.

If not, then you could default on a payment to either one or both of these two companies. This will result in more fees from both the creditor and the company whose payment was rejected. Additionally, the company whose payment is rejected will receive notice that your card has been declined.

Rest assured, you do not want any of these associated with you, your payment history with the company, or your credit file.

Remember to account for all automatic charges.

After you have established some credit, you will be a more desirable borrower. That does not mean, however, that you should go crazy and load up with loans and credit cards.

There will always be things you need, and often when you least expect it. It can prove to be good practice to leave a bit of wiggle room between what the lender offers and what you accept.

True Story:

A sad, true story of this happening with life-altering results is the real estate situation that unfolded around 2008.

In short, far too many people were approved for either mortgages or refinance opportunities that they could not afford when compared to their income and other expenses.

Unfortunately, a number of borrowers were offered more than they could afford, and they took it. Even though in many cases, they didn't need it. Here is a hypothetical example of this tragic, real-life story.

We have a couple looking to buy a house for $100,000. They want low payments, around $350–$400, to keep everything manageable and have money in case of emergencies. They are considering the total amount as well as the monthly payment.

At the bank, the lender joyfully announces that they are approved for $175,000. Their monthly payment will be $500 and make things tight. But, excited about the possibilities, they decide to find a way to make it work.

They return to the housing market with their letter of approval and a new perspective, one that sets their sights on a place for $175,000.

However, what they did not consider was how using all of the money they were approved for would take them beyond their means.

Sadly, this is not uncommon. Because they trusted the lender who told them they were approved, they ceased to consider the overall costs. And when focusing solely on the payment, they believed they could make it.

The couple made the purchase for $175,000, despite knowing it would put them in a financial bind if any one thing went wrong.

And it did.

When everything caught up to itself, many who were approved for debt beyond their means lost their homes.

Countless homeowners were forced to sell and take a loss; others went into foreclosure. And even after losing that home, many are still digging themselves out from the financial mess it created over a decade later.

While many borrowers may be uninformed, they should not simply go along with the lender's suggestions. After all, lenders are in the business of making money.

You are in the business of building a sound, secure financial future for yourself.

Borrowers cannot rely on the excuse that they didn't know or understand something when the bill comes due. Lack of knowledge does not make the problem go away, nor does it protect from having to make good on the financial obligation.

So before you borrow, do your homework.

Honor your responsibilities. Know your limits and focus on the amount you are borrowing plus the cost, rather than whether or not you can afford to make the monthly payment.

Yes, both details matter. But focusing entirely on the monthly payment is an excellent way to overlook the true cost of what you are borrowing. This is often how people wind up in worse situations than anticipated.

Revisit chapter 9, example (f), on page 56. Pay attention to the section about making only the minimum payment and notice how the interest adds up over time. Now, envision not being able to make that payment.

Life is uncertain and financial situations come and go. Be realistic and base your decisions on what makes the best sense to reduce, not increase, your financial stress and worry.

SUMMARY:
GET STARTED

Remember to only borrow what you need.
Review these options and get started:

» Auto loans

» Credit cards: department store, retailer, major bank card

» Personal loans

» Student loans

» Watch out for over-spending & over-extending

Chapter 11

CREDIT SCORES & CUR

Your credit score and credit utilization ratio or rate (CUR) will be vital to the quality of your financial options throughout your life. Let's examine them for a better understanding.

Credit Scores

By now, you know that credit scores are very important when applying for any form of credit.

The higher your credit score, the lower your rates, higher your credit lines or loan amount (with supporting income), and the better your overall chances of being approved.

In general, credit scores are based on the popular scoring software created by the Fair Isaac Corporation (FICO), and range from 300–850.

Companies use different ranges and methods of determining the score, so it can be difficult to pinpoint your exact number. Regardless of how they do it, the lower the borrower's score, the harder it is to borrow money.

You might be surprised to learn that you could have more than one credit score. This would be due to the fact that lenders use different scores for different products. And, there are different formulas for determining credit scores and multiple credit reporting sources.

This could explain why you might qualify for various rates for the same loan when applying to a few creditors. Therefore, the possibility of the lower rate is a solid argument as to why you would want to shop around.

Credit scores are based on the information found on credit reports, which is why it is important to review them for accuracy. However, credit scores are generally not provided on credit reports. And although some creditors will provide them for free, there are instances where you might have to pay a fee to receive your credit score.

Credit Score Breakdown

The credit score range varies between systems but can be broken down for general understanding. Keep in mind that a low credit score is common for individuals who either lack a positive credit history or have never established any credit. But with enough timely payments, that will change.

Following is the general breakdown and how a creditor sees a potential borrower from the first glance at their score. There are several factors they will consider, but this is where they begin.

Score Range	Rating	Borrowing Ability & Strength	Will They Pay?
800+	Excellent	Easy/Very Strong	Yes
740–799	Very Good	Better than Average	Yes
670–739	Good	Average	Probably
580–669	Fair	Less than Average	Maybe
≤ 579	Poor	Very Difficult/Weak	Possibly Not

The lowest ratings have the most challenges when it comes to borrowing, but remember, not all low scores are due to poor payment or borrowing habits. When a creditor reviews the credit report, they will see which factors played a role in establishing the credit score.

As previously mentioned, life takes its twists and turns, often leaving people in financial predicaments. At that point, many find themselves needing to fix their credit, which is usually harder to do than maintaining it.

Because no one can predict the future, I urge you to take the time to build a solid, dependable payment pattern from the beginning.

If you ever find yourself in the position of having to defend yourself against unforeseen financial pitfalls, your credit history could be the one thing that rescues you.

Variables & Credit Utilization Ratio (CUR)

There are several variables that can, and will, affect your credit score. Keep an eye on those you have the most control over to ensure the highest score possible, but understand that your credit score will always fluctuate.

Here are the most common variables, (list not all-inclusive):

» How close you are to your credit limit per account

» How long you have had your credit accounts;

» How many & which types of credit accounts you have;

» Number of credit inquiries;

» Payment timeliness; and

» Your credit utilization ratio or rate (CUR).

Credit utilization ratio pertains to how much credit you currently have available through your open revolving credit lines and how much you currently owe. This is applied to accounts individually as well as collectively.

Your total CUR is determined by taking the existing balance total from all lines of credit and dividing it by your total credit limit. The resulting number should total less than 10% and absolutely no more than 30%.

Example:

Let's refer to the accounts and available credit lines in example (d) of chapter 7 (page 41), for a better understanding of CUR.

First, we'll use the initial credit lines and place a balance on each of the credit cards. For DS CC, the credit line is $2,000 with a balance owed of $500 and for MJ CC, there is a credit line of $10,000 and a balance of $2,000. The student loan is not a revolving line of credit and does not apply to the credit utilization ratio, so we will ignore it for this discussion.

In this first situation using these details, the CUR is 21%, which is less than the 30%, but more than the preferred 10%.

This percentage is arrived at by taking the *total outstanding debt* of $2,500 and dividing it by the *total available credit* of $12,000 (2,500 ÷ 12,000 = .21).

Second, we'll refer to the same example but use the amounts *after* adjusting the credit lines with the same outstanding balances. Therefore, we have the new credit line for DS CC of $500 with a balance owed of $500, and for MJ CC, the new credit line of $4,000 with a balance owed of $2,000.

We ignore the student and auto loans because neither are revolving lines of credit.

Once again, we divide the *total outstanding debt* by the *total available credit* and find that the new credit utilization ratio is 56% (2,500 ÷ 4,500 = .56). What a difference.

As you can see in both cases, the CUR is less than desirable.

Additionally, and this is particularly noteworthy for new borrowers to understand, when looking at the CUR for DS CC or if it were your only line of credit at $500, you would be hurting. Because if so, with an outstanding balance of $500, the CUR would be an uncompromising, full-scale 100% (500 ÷ 500 = 1.0).

This is not what you want.

And before applying for any other credit, this account must be either paid off or the debt considerably reduced to improve your CUR.

This example is shown here in the table. Take a minute to look it over.

Credit Card	Balance	Credit Line	CUR
DS CC	$500	$2,000	0.25 (25%)
MJ CC	$2,000	$10,000	0.20 (20%)
Totals	**$2,500**	**$12,000**	**0.21 (21%)**
After Credit Line Adjustments			
DS CC	$500	$500	1.0 (100%)
MJ CC	$2,000	$4,000	.50 (50%)
New Totals	**$2,500**	**$4,500**	**.56 (56%)**

Closing An Account

Throughout the beginning stages of building your credit, you probably won't need to close accounts. However, as time passes, you will either prefer something else or won't need an account.

As previously shown in the discussion about CUR, it is important to not jeopardize your credit when closing an account. Realize that by having one open credit card rather than two can hurt your CUR, not help it.

Even if the balance is only on one card, having two open accounts allows for your total available credit amount to be higher. And this directly influences your total credit utilization ratio.

While thinking about closing an account, review the details. An important factor to consider is how long an account has been open.

Longevity with a creditor speaks favorably of you and your loyalty to a company. The longer you have the account and remain in good standing, the better your score.

Closing an account requires scrutiny and wise use of credit.

When you are established enough to qualify, the same rule applies to transferring balances. Taking advantage frequently can hinder your credit score if you repeatedly close the accounts after transferring from them.

Think twice when making a major move. Remember that creditors seldom know you personally and rely heavily on the information gleaned from your credit file.

Understanding how to work with your accounts, while knowing which ones benefit you and how, will be instrumental in building an excellent credit history and admirable credit score.

SUMMARY:
CREDIT SCORES & CUR

Reach a high credit score and keep it there by applying these tips:

» Keep track of your CUR

» Maintain lower balances; do not max out credit lines

» Pay all bills on time

» Understand how credit scores are determined

» Use discretion when closing accounts

Chapter 12

CREDIT DISPUTES

No one wants to have credit issues. And this is especially true when starting to build credit. But there may come a time when you will, so let's cover the basics.

A credit dispute is when you discover an inaccuracy or error on your credit report and address it for correction.

What To Look For

Review your credit report carefully and highlight or circle any errors. Confirm the correct details and then address the issue(s) immediately. As described earlier in chapter 6, errors can often be fixed with a call to the creditor, followed by a letter to the credit bureaus.

If you find negative information that is correct but past the legal time allowed, then it must be addressed. This type of error requires supporting documentation along with a letter requesting the correction.

However, if the incorrect entries on your report are not yours, they could be indicators of identity theft.

These items require immediate attention. If they are fraudulent, a written request might not be enough to get the job done. Therefore, it's wise to begin the process of correcting errors as soon as possible to prevent further issues.

In the case of fraud or identity theft, professional assistance might be required.

In general, look for any of the following:

» Address(es) not yours or wrong address;

» Bankruptcies (not yours or past their time frame);

» Delinquent accounts or payments;

» Duplicate accounts (sold loans often get posted more than once);

» False inquiries;

» Fraudulent accounts (they are not yours);

» Inaccurate account balance or status;

» Inaccurate credit line or loan amount;

» Incorrect received or required payment amount;

» Late payments that were paid on time;

» Missing accounts; and

» Misspelled name(s).

As you can see, there are a lot of reasons to periodically check your credit report. And if you do find an inaccuracy, what's next?

How to move forward after finding an error will depend on what it is and who provided the information to the credit bureau. While you're at it, check all three credit bureau reports to see if they all show the same error(s).

Fixing Credit Report Errors

I would be remiss if I did not stress the importance of documenting communication in reference to your accounts. Therefore, whenever discussing accounts, take notes of the conversation.

Notes should include at minimum: the date of the call, to whom you spoke, and the details of the conversation including any promised solution. If any correspondence takes place by text, take screenshots and save them. By email? Save them in a dedicated file on your phone or computer.

You never know when you will need to prove or verify facts or details about an account. The more supporting documentation you have in the case of any questions, the better.

After reviewing your report and finding what appears to be an error, confirm the facts and check previous notes about your accounts. Is it indeed an error? If so, then go forward with the necessary process.

There are times when the issue in question is simply a typo. Maybe there's a misspelled street address or wrong middle initial for your name. Often, these can be easily cleared up with a written request to the credit bureau that has the incorrect detail.

If the error is with a particular creditor, also known as a furnisher, then start there. Call them first and discuss the discrepancy. Assuming they acknowledge the error is theirs, ask them to correct the account. Then request a letter identifying the necessary correction be sent to you and to the credit bureau(s) to whom they had provided the information.

When a creditor determines an error is frivolous, they could choose not to research it further. If so, they must notify you in writing within five days of their determination.

Occasionally, a creditor will require time to look into the matter. If that is the case, ask them to respond to you in writing within the legally allowed time of thirty days.

If you do not receive a response after a week or so, follow up to make sure they are completing their investigation. Stay on top of it. If they are not responding, connect with a supervisor for resolution. Request written confirmation of their findings and again, ask for corrections to be sent to the credit bureaus. Document all correspondence.

When an error pertains to correct negative information but the allowed time frame has expired, then request to have it removed. This will take a bit of effort on your part, but your credit is worth it.

Before submitting your written request to the applicable credit agency, make a copy of all supporting documentation proving your case. When you have it all together, include it with your credit dispute letter, and send it by certified mail.

Retain copies of all correspondence pertaining to credit reports and accounts.

Credit Dispute Letters

A credit dispute letter is what you send when disputing a discrepancy on your credit report, possibly to both the creditor and credit bureau.

For the credit bureau, you can complete this process online. If you choose this method, take screenshots, save emails, and carefully document all electronic communications. However, in the past and as is still widely practiced, it has been advised to send a printed letter via certified mail.

This allows you to have a copy for your records, a time-stamped receipt, and a record of the bureau's receipt of your letter upon delivery. Again, keep these items in your file for reference.

Okay, you've decided to send a letter. But what to write and before sealing the envelope, what to include?

There are two examples of credit dispute letters provided for reference at the end of this chapter. One is structured toward the creditor and the other is for the credit bureau. Read them both and tweak whichever one suits your needs for where you are in the process.

When you have gathered all supporting documentation, including the findings from the creditor (if applicable), make copies of everything. Include a copy of the portion of your credit report that contains the error(s). Circle the errors.

Next, write a letter to the bureau and provide all details. If using the examples provided in this guide, substitute items in the brackets with your details.

Package it up and send it via certified mail, preferably with return receipt requested. Any questions on how to complete this part of the process can be answered by the post office, but do fill everything out as instructed.

The credit bureau has thirty days to research and respond to your inquiry. If all goes well, you will receive a favorable response and hopefully see an increase on your credit score within a few weeks. Unless, of course, it was a simple typo or other detail that does not impact a score.

However, if your dispute is rejected, you may appeal their decision. If you pursue this option, you will send your appeal to the Consumer Financial Protection Bureau.

The package to them will include at least everything previously sent to the bureau along with the bureau's response and any other information that will help your case. If the bureau failed to respond within the allowed time frame, provide that information as well.

This is when having the return receipt from the certified mail could be handy.

But don't stop there. Do your research to confirm you have everything you need.

If your appeal is also rejected, then you can submit a brief statement explaining the situation. Although this will not improve your credit score or rectify the situation, it will be posted for future potential creditors to see.

In some cases, this statement could make the difference between denial and approval. On that note then, it doesn't hurt to try.

Example (g): Sample Dispute Letter to Creditor (replace bracket details with yours)

Via Certified Mail

[Date]

[Company or Individual]
[Address]
[City, State, Zip]

Re: **[Your Name]**
[Account Number, Case File Number, etc.]

Dear Sir/Madam:

I discovered inaccurate information on my credit file that [you or your company] provided to [name credit bureau]. I am writing to dispute it and have circled the [error(s)] on a portion of the copy of my report, enclosed.

Referencing the above mentioned [account, case number, etc.], the [name the error] is [incorrect or incomplete]. The correct information is [provide details]. Please have this [removed *(if entirely inaccurate)* or corrected *(if applicable)*].

(If you have more than one error with this provider, include a new paragraph for each error and its details.)

I have enclosed [a copy or copies] of [supporting documentation, such as payment records, loan agreement with payment details, court documents, lien releases, etc.] supporting my request. Please investigate the [issue(s)] indicated and contact the credit reporting companies to have [it or them] [deleted or corrected] as soon as possible.

Please advise if you require more information. If not, then please send confirmation of the corrections to me at the address provided below.

Thank you for your assistance,

(Sign your name here)

[Your First and Last Name, Printed]
[Your Address]
[Your City, State, Zip]
[Your Phone Number with Area Code]

Enclosures: [list enclosed item(s) here]

Example (h): Sample Dispute Letter to Credit Bureau (replace bracket details with yours)

Via Certified Mail

[Date]

[Credit Bureau]
Complaint Department
[Address]
[City, State, Zip]

Re: [Your Name]
[Credit Report Confirmation Number (if available)]

Dear Sir/Madam:

I have reviewed my credit file and am writing to request the following [correction(s)]. I have circled the [error(s)] on a portion of the copy of my report, enclosed.

The [name the error] [provided by (*name the company, individual or institution listed for giving the information to the bureau, if applicable*)] is [incorrect or incomplete]. Please [remove (if entirely inaccurate) or correct (if applicable)]. The correct information is [provide details].

(If you have more than one error where a provider is being identified, include a new paragraph for each error and its provider and details.)

I have enclosed [a copy or copies] of [supporting documentation, such as payment records, loan agreement with payment details, court documents, lien releases, etc.] supporting my request. Please investigate the [issue(s)] indicated and [delete or correct] [it or them] as soon as possible.

Please advise if you require more information.

Thank you for your assistance,

(Sign your name here)

[Your First and Last Name, Printed]
[Your Address]
[Your City, State, Zip]
[Your Phone Number with Area Code]

Enclosures: [list enclosed item(s) here]

SUMMARY:
CREDIT DISPUTES

Correct errors on your credit report immediately:

» Check credit report for accuracy & errors

» Contact creditor first if errors were reported by them

» Follow up with creditor & credit bureau

» If necessary, file appropriate dispute letter(s)

» Make & keep copies of all correspondence in writing

Chapter 13

CREDIT THREATS

As much as I hate to acknowledge it, anyone can be a victim of credit threats and identity theft.

Credit threats are constantly changing and multiplying, making it impossible to include them all here. However, the information provided in this chapter should bring awareness to their reality and encourage caution. All threats involve some form of identity theft and could include:

- » Mail or online fraud;
- » SIM swap fraud;
- » Skimming & shimming;
- » Social engineering; and
- » Unauthorized charges.

An important note to stress is that of familiar names and faces. Even though someone may be your spouse, relative, or best friend, that does not exclude them from being possible threats to your credit.

Exercise caution if anyone asks to borrow your credit card.

If you want to help someone who asks to borrow your credit card, make the purchase yourself and have them repay you. This might sound a bit extreme, however, once they have your information, they could use it later without your knowledge or approval. And if they do, this could create debt and other costly problems for which you could be held accountable.

Having granted them permission in the past to use your card could void the validity of your dispute, therefore making you the responsible party. In such cases, if you contact your creditor to dispute the unauthorized charge(s), you might be asked to sign a sworn statement.

Although we all want to trust our family and friends with our lives and first born, it is best not to trust them with our personal details. Individuals privy to such information could, at any time, access your credit and steal your identity. This is an even stronger possibility if you no longer speak to each other.

I have two acquaintances who suffered identity theft from college roommates with whom they no longer associate. Therefore, please heed this warning.

Mail Or Online Fraud

Fraud is not restricted to someone physically stealing your credit card. Nor is it possible to guarantee foolproof protection from fraud. However, you can take precautions to protect yourself, and you should.

Mail fraud is committed most commonly by mail theft. If a thief retrieves information from your mail, they could have access to your credit and accounts. It's impossible to monitor all activity, but implementing the following will reduce their opportunities for success.

First, always check all of your mail, even the junk mail. Many credit offers arrive with all of your information preprinted, which can be an open door for a thief. Either shred or burn all pieces with personal information on it that you do not want.

Second, are you moving? Be sure to notify the post office when you change your address. Contact all creditors and financial institutions and provide them with the new address, preferably at least twenty days before your next billing statement. This is important, even if you receive all statements electronically.

Note that if you do not receive your bill, you will still be expected to pay on time. If your bill is late, contact the company to make sure they have the correct address and that it has been sent. Confirm your due date and the amount owed, in case the bill does not arrive.

In addition, if you pay bills by mail, do not leave payments in your mailbox or an unsecured location, such as a hotel or building lobby. Always drop them off at the post office or into a secure mailbox.

Third, there is an option available through the U.S. Postal Service, referred to as Informed Delivery® by USPS®.

This is a free mail-monitoring service currently available to those with a qualifying residential address. One of the service's primary goals is to thwart mail and identity theft. Because only one email address can be assigned to a physical address, make sure it is yours.

A mailbox is vulnerable when it is physically accessible to all. Anyone can complete credit applications or place orders using that address.

If a thief claims your address with their email, they can see the mail activity for your address. Now they will know when items they ordered using your address and credit are scheduled for delivery. This allows the thief to pick up the items without you ever knowing they exist.

They can also see when packages *you* have ordered will be delivered. Therefore, if they are not credit thieves, they could still be monitoring your mail to steal your packages.

If this service interests you or someone you know, visit their website to learn more and if qualified, complete the process. At the time of this writing, the information can be found at: InformedDelivery.USPS.com.

Online fraud consists of thieves obtaining and/or using your credit card information online. Note that whether you choose to bank or shop on the Internet is irrelevant to whether or not you could become a victim of online fraud.

Do not be fooled into believing that because you don't indulge in the conveniences of online services, others will not. In fact, expect the contrary. The Internet is the preferred place to use your credit information because identification and signatures are not required to make purchases online.

SIM Swap Fraud

This form of identity theft is particularly tricky to trace. It will probably require professional assistance to resolve, possibly from the FBI or other law enforcement agencies.

SIM swap fraud is where the thief acquires access to the victim's accounts by way of their cell phone number and personal data.

Some speculate this is accomplished through public or unsecured Internet connections. However, several cases have proven that hackers have used social media platforms and cellular service providers to steal an individual's cell phone number.

And everything attached to it.

Take a moment to think about your online presence and the information you share. Remember when you set up your account and the process requested a phone number? If you used your cell, then someone with your cell phone number could now have access to that account.

Granted, having access to your social media account might not concern you, but realistically, it does not stop there. This same phone number is likely to be used on all of your online accounts, such as credit cards, banks, banking apps, etc.

As for social media, now they have access to all of your contacts, friends, and family members. Any information your contacts have posted for friends to see, the hacker now has access to. They can also pose as you and ask seemingly innocent questions of your contacts.

So, how does it work?

A hacker will start by gathering personal data from online accounts. Sometimes they select someone in particular, such as a celebrity or someone with a valuable social media handle, but anyone could be a target. When they have enough information to be able to pose as their victim, they are ready to move forward with stealing the phone number.

The thief can contact the carrier and tell the representative they have lost their SIM card and need to activate a new one. The rep will ask for the cell phone number and confirm identity with information such as an email address and answers to security questions on the account.

Thieves do their homework. They are prepared to answer personal questions relative to an account.

Upon completion of this brief confirmation, the rep transfers the cell number to the SIM card the thief has in their possession. The victim's cell phone no longer receives calls or messages.

Therefore, all calls, texts, and voice messages will go to the hacker's phone, including those used for the two-step authentication process. When you consider how quickly someone can access and manipulate accounts online with the correct information, you can see the danger of this threat.

When a financial institution senses unusual activity on an account, they generally confirm the transaction with the customer (or here, the victim). The transactions they question will appear to be abnormal per the account holder's spending habits. Maybe something like a $10,000 purchase on a credit card or $20,000 transfer from one account to another.

And, who will receive the text or email inquiring if the transaction is legitimate? The hacker who initiated the transaction in question. As you can see, this form of theft creates serious and potentially costly problems on many levels for the victim.

Skimming & Shimming

Credit card skimming and shimming both require the use of the physical credit card. Places where your card can be skimmed or shimmed include anywhere you use the card. And all that's required is a dishonest individual who can access it or a terminal that has the skimmer or shimmer installed.

Skimming and shimming require a device that reads the account number and information from the credit card itself. Skimming reads the magnetic stripe while shimming retrieves information from the EMV chip credit cards.

Skimming devices are easier to identify because the card reader may appear to have been tampered with, but shimming devices are much harder to detect. The primary indicator of a shimmer's presence is resistance when inserting the card into the chip-reading terminal.

When the card has been skimmed or shimmed, the information can be used for phone and Internet purchases. Your information could also be sold to create counterfeit cards.

In the case of counterfeit cards, your card would still work and unless the creditor contacts you, you would not be alarmed. However, when reviewing your statement, you would discover the fraudulent, unauthorized charges.

Often, by the time you see the charges, the counterfeit card will have been discarded for a new one. Regardless, you must report the fraudulent activity and request a new card and account number from your creditor.

Always use caution and be willing to refuse the credit transaction if you suspect anything unusual.

Social Engineering

Social engineering is the term applied to methods used to obtain information from victims. The information criminals seek includes passwords, account numbers or details, names, addresses, and more.

As mentioned earlier with online fraud, social engineering can be used regardless of an individual's online activity status. Scams used today are sophisticated and create easy traps to fall in to. Sadly, everyone is a potential victim and therefore, everyone should use caution when revealing their details.

Phishing is a method of obtaining your information through emails that has become increasingly common.

The most widely used emails for this form of theft resemble or imitate emails from financial institutions. They are deceptive in that they have bank logos, images, and web addresses that you would expect to see from your legitimate institution.

Opening the email does not necessarily expose you to identity theft. However, responding to it probably will. If you can identify it as a fake prior to opening (by hovering over the sender's details), then do not open it.

Instead, contact the institution they are claiming to be. Call them or go directly to their website to ask where and how to forward the fake email.

Next, forward the phishing email to the institution and allow them to begin an investigation. Now, after having sent the email to their security division, mark the email as spam and finally, delete.

Note that emails from your financial institution will not ask for any personal information.

If you do open the email and click on any links, you will be directed to the scammer's website and instructed to provide your details. Such details can include your account number(s), passwords, and personal information. When they have your information, they can empty your account(s).

As you can see, these emails are not to be toyed with or taken lightly.

Do not click on any links.
Do not reply or provide any information.

Smishing is one of the latest methods of social engineering to take on a life of its own. This method is conducted through text messages. A similar approach is used as with phishing, and because it is quick and easy, many people respond before questioning its validity.

Text messages are generally trusted because they usually come from our contact list. This is the power of smishing because most people will reply to messages and click on links and phone numbers in a text from a peer.

However, caution must always be used. If links and phone numbers are provided within the text in question, never click on them. Alternatively, exit the message and open a new browser window to visit the website directly, or find your statement (if applicable), and call the number(s) found there.

In addition, note that the simple act of replying "STOP" to texts can be a trigger. And if someone you know sends an unusual text to what they typically send, call them directly and ask if it is from them.

Texts and messages from familiar contacts containing only a link or similar often come from scammers.

Vishing (voice phishing), is another method of social engineering used to deceive and gain access to information. Although most people are aware of telephone scams, some have become quite sophisticated and sound legitimate.

Always be leery of calls from at least the following:

» Anyone claiming you have won something (especially if you have not entered to win anything);

» Anyone concerned you have not updated your computer's software;

» Anyone demanding to be paid with gift cards or cash;

» Government entities threatening to freeze your accounts; and

» Utility companies threatening to cut off service if you do not pay them immediately (especially in gift cards or cash).

Be smart. Think logically. Slow down and do not panic.

These calls are designed to intimidate. By creating a sense of urgency, it is easier for the caller to elicit valuable information from you. Do not tell them anything.

> ***Be suspicious of unusual emails, texts, or phone calls.***
> ***Do not provide information, but call the entity or contact directly.***

Unauthorized Charges

If your card has been lost or stolen, borrowed and not returned, misplaced, or out of your possession in any other way, contact your creditor immediately and report it as lost. Most companies have customer service lines that never close for lost or stolen cards. The sooner you act, the less opportunity exists for unauthorized charges to wind up on your account.

Any and all unauthorized charges must be reported to the creditor as soon as you discover them. It doesn't matter if the card is still in your possession or the purchases were made online. It only matters that you did not authorize the purchase(s).

The first thing to do is immediately contact the credit card company. Take notes of the call, including: the date, to whom you speak, the activity in question, action you are required to take, and the outcome of the call.

Discuss your financial responsibilities with the creditor. Again, if the purchases were made by someone who had been granted permission to use your card before, the rules may be different.

However, in many cases, you could have zero liability for the charge(s). In others, depending on the circumstances, you might be responsible for up to $50, per the Fair Credit Billing Act. Always ask about the specifics for your account.

Follow the call with any instructions provided by your creditor. Additionally, consider sending a letter to your creditor outlining the fraudulent activity. Include a copy of your statement and highlight the unauthorized charge(s). Maintain a copy of all correspondence for your records.

Protect Your Identity

Although it is impossible to protect yourself entirely from identity theft, please consider using precautions. Here are a few suggestions:

- Change passwords frequently;
- Limit personal information & details posted to social media;
- Refrain from using unsecured Internet connections;
- Request a different method for two-step authentication;
- Try not to use cell phone numbers on accounts; and
- Use virtual credit card numbers or equivalent for online purchases.

If you are a victim of identity theft, you are entitled to a free copy of your credit report, per the Fair Credit Reporting Act. In addition, you may wish to place a fraud alert on your credit report. Discuss it with the credit agency if you want to pursue this option.

Also, be sure to contact your state to learn of possible reporting laws that could provide additional rights. To find this information, begin with government agencies in your area.

An excellent option to use when you are *not* seeking new credit, is a credit freeze. Placing a credit freeze on your credit file makes it impossible for anyone to access your credit report.

A credit freeze is initiated by you with the credit bureaus directly. When you exercise this option, be forewarned to keep any codes or passwords the credit bureau gives you. These codes or passwords will be the only way back into your credit.

Keep all credit report details, information, and passwords in a protected place that only you can access.

Note that although a credit freeze will thwart attempts to open new accounts in your name, it will not prevent identity theft or unauthorized use of existing accounts. But if you won't need more credit for a while, it's an acceptable way to attempt to protect your identity and credit.

I know this is a lot to absorb, but hopefully it brings awareness and validity to the importance of monitoring and protecting your credit.

And although I don't mention online apps for monitoring credit, credit card activity, banking, or anything else related to finances, I know many will prefer the conveniences they provide. In fact, you may find some particularly useful for masking your identity when making online purchases.

However you choose to handle your online activity, please keep in mind what has been discussed. Remember to check statements frequently and review your credit report thoroughly at least once a year.

If you have been or are experiencing identity theft, please take this seriously. For complete information on what to do, go to IdentityTheft.gov to begin the recovery process.

SUMMARY:
CREDIT THREATS

Be proactive to thwart identity theft. Do what you can:

» Be aware of surroundings and suspicious individuals; never leave purse or wallet unattended

» Confirm receipt of your card back from public transactions

» Do not lend your credit card or account information

» Do not provide personal or account information in emails, text messages or phone calls that you do not initiate

» Implement a fraud alert and/or credit freeze when appropriate

» Monitor statement activity frequently

» Report all unauthorized charges or suspicious activity to creditor(s)

» Use secure and trusted websites for online payments

» Use virtual credit card numbers or equivalent

Conclusion

Congratulations! You've made it through the entire guide. I hope you read it thoroughly and revisit it often.

At this point, you should have a better understanding of and be more comfortable with at least the following:

» Application process & pre-application prep;

» Common credit terms & vocabulary;

» Credit disputes;

» Credit lines & loans;

» Determining factors in credit scores & getting approved;

» How to get started in building credit;

» How to maintain a healthy credit score;

» Importance of budgeting & timely payments;

» Importance of credit, credit scores & CUR;

» Ordering, reading & understanding credit reports;

» Protecting your credit & identity; and

» What to look for in a creditor.

And, although there are a variety of topics covered here, there is always more to learn. In general, yes, but also per situation.

Every account, every detail, every payment, and every person's history all play parts in building a credit history. It's impossible to guarantee any one situation will be exactly as another.

Therefore, it is everyone's responsibility to educate themselves on available options and whether or not they fit their needs and situation.

Remember that this is a beginner's guide. Please continue to research and expand your knowledge on topics of interest when you need to learn more.

Know that by laying a solid foundation for your credit today, you stand a much better chance of having a solid credit score in your near future.

And with that, well, what can I say?

Your future awaits, so start building!

Wishing you all the best in your financial success,

Kendyl

ABOUT THE AUTHOR

Kendyl Jameson currently writes of her experiences and what she has learned from them. She hopes that by sharing her stories, readers are empowered to live their best lives.

In addition to *DIY Credit Builder: Beginners' Guide to Building Credit*, she has written *DIY Credit Repair: Beginners' Guide to Credit Repair*, also available in Spanish, *DIY Reparación de Crédito: Guía del principiante para la reparación del crédito.*

These guides are intended to help others build, fix, and maintain a healthy credit score, while learning how to understand and manage one's finances.

Her work also includes *The Pirates of My Soul: A Transformational Voyage to Self-Empowerment.* This memoir encapsulates her relationships, wherein she shares personal observations and analysis with readers. Her story is revealing and empowering while touching on relatable topics.

If you like her work, please leave a review on Amazon (where all books may be purchased), and Goodreads.com.

Learn more about her books and follow Kendyl on Amazon. Visit the links below or scan the QR code to go directly to Kendyl's author page.

Facebook.com/KendylJameson
KendylJameson.com
@KendylJameson

Made in United States
Troutdale, OR
11/03/2026

56845104R00060